D0649596

A PROPER GARDEN

A Proper Garden

ON
PERENNIALS
IN THE
BORDER

ELISABETH SHELDON

STACKPOLE
BOOKS

Published by
STACKPOLE BOOKS
Cameron and Kelker Streets
P.O. Box 1831
Harrisburg, PA 17105

Printed in the United States of America

10 9 8 7 6 5 4 3

Earlier versions of "A Proper Garden," "Hardy Geraniums," "Campanulas," "Plant
Names," "Salvias," "Almost All About Windflowers," and "Lavender" were published
in *American Horticulturist*, the magazine of the American Horticultural Society,
7931 Boulevard Drive, Alexandria, VA 22308. Copyright © February 1985,
October 1987, April 1988, June 1988, December 1988, April 1989, and June 1989
respectively. Reprinted by permission.

Earlier versions of "Dianthus," "Rock Plants," and "Sterling Silver" were published
in *Horticulture, The Magazine of American Gardening,* 20 Park Plaza, Suite 1220,
Boston, MA 02116. Copyright © 1985, 1987, 1987, respectively, Horticulture
Partners. Reprinted by permission.

Design by Tracy Patterson
Illustrations by Constance Sheldon and George Sheldon

Library of Congress Cataloging-in-Publication Data

Sheldon, Elisabeth.
   A proper garden: on perennials in the border/Elisabeth Sheldon.
   p.   cm.
   ISBN 0-8117-0553-6
   1. Perennials.   2. Garden borders.   3. Gardening.   I. Title.
SB434.S52   1989
635.9'32–dc19
                                               88-38732
                                                  CIP

To Audrey Harkness O'Connor:
scholar, horticulturist, and an inspiration
to all who know her

CONTENTS

FOREWORD

It was, i think, the heroine, Laurie, in Rose Macauley's famous *The Towers of Trebizond* who complained (when on a journey there and contemplating the very same thing) "that everyone nowadays is writing their Turkey books."

Today everyone is writing their garden books and happy plagiarism is rife; it is fascinating to any garden book buff to meet the same phrase out from the mouths of very different babes and sucklings, as the Bible has it. X coined it, Y pinched it, Z adapted it and none of them, one fears, has actually grown the plant so eloquently described.

Elisabeth Sheldon, I hasten to add, is not in that company. She reads voraciously and practices equally. She knows intimately the plants she writes about. She goes through the fire that all real proprietorial gardeners experience (and I believe it impossible for committed gardeners *not* to be proprietorial): the discovery of a seemingly exquisite plant as described, say, by Reginald Farrer; the enquiry into its cultivation by the accepted authorities—Graham Thomas, perhaps, or Alan Bloom; the study of its friends and relations from the R.H.S. Dictionary and *Hortus Third*, only to find that the latter tome (usually fine) actually fails to list it. A further realisation emphasises what is known only too well: far too many of those garden gurus practice their art in a very different environment. England is not New England and Elisabeth Sheldon's zone 5 Finger Lakes garden has a climate which she rightly describes as manic-depressive; she does not write from or for Surrey. *A Proper Garden* then (the title itself is a sly dig against the only too prevalent blandness of the North American foundation planting and mulch syndrome which is often, one suspects, a convenient excuse to avoid work, both mental and physical) is concerned above all to encourage individual gardeners throughout North America to develop a garden aesthetic of their own. This does not mean reinventing every horticultural wheel but trying it, adapting it, using it and, above all, enjoying the process. Mrs. Sheldon tries a coveted plant again and again before giving in, and as her own garden amply demonstrates, usually it decides to make itself at home. If only the *Acanthus spinosus* which she kindly gave me a couple of years ago would be equally so in my presumably warmer zone 6 garden. But then zonitis is a national disease she avoids like the plague it is.

Elisabeth Sheldon is in the traditional line of acerbic lady gardeners—which began with Jane Loudon and Gertrude Jekyll, and continues through Katharine White and Eleanor Perenji—who are determined to share their personal vision of paradise. She says out loud many of the things we have ourselves thought but were either too polite or just plain chicken to say (dead daylily flowers can indeed look like wet socks on a laundry line). Such a fresh eye is necessary for it helps us to keep our own eyes skinned for the banal and the bad and more importantly for the good and the serendipitous in an art form which is available to anyone, anywhere, with a few square yards of soil to play in.

Allen Paterson
Director, Royal Botanical Gardens
Hamilton, Ontario

INTRODUCTION

"IT'S TIME WE STOPPED FEELING sorry for ourselves," said a gardening friend of mine, "time we stopped whimpering about all the plants other people can raise that we can't. This is a *good* place to garden. Look at all the things we can grow!"

At this she cast her eyes appreciatively over the garden we were standing in, expressing such delight that I felt ashamed of begrudging gardeners in more benign climates their luck.

Since having been thus chidden, I've been working on my gratitude. I can't say I've succeeded one hundred percent but I am making progress. I remind myself of gardeners who are worse off than we Northeasterners like the relative in Nebraska who had to raise tomato plants in tubs under her one tree (a cottonwood poplar) because they couldn't stand the broiling sun and tearing prairie winds. And what about people in Saskatchewan? Things could always be worse.

Most of us gardeners have problems and limitations unimaginable to garden writers who live in Europe and other meteorologically blessed spots. Their garden books are educational in many ways and often amusing, but rarely do they help us cope with our special situations.

Today is the twenty-second of December. In the early part of the month we had mild temperatures and continuous rain. Then, abruptly, the thermometer dropped into the teens. The wet earth froze into stalagmites, little brown mountain peaks like the ones in medieval paintings. The small plants that had been set out in late summer were clinging to these stalagmites, their poor roots waving in the wind. There was no way of helping them until the ground thawed again, which it did a few days ago. I trudged around in boots, poking young plants back down in the mud and covering them with jars until I ran out of jars. We will continue to have freezes and thaws until May. The plants will be pushed up by the earth and down by me all winter and spring, and only the toughest will survive. Mind you, I'm not complaining. After living here for fifteen years, I might have learned better than to set out small plants in late summer. And I wouldn't have, if I'd had more room in the cold frame.

E.S.
December 1988

Rosa gallica officinalis (apothecary's rose)

Most of us gardeners have problems and limitations unimaginable to garden writers who live in Europe and other meteorologically blessed spots.

1

A PROPER GARDEN

SOME YEARS AGO MY HUSBAND, George, and I decided that after many years of moving about, we wanted to settle down permanently. We had always gardened here and there but we longed to own a large piece of land, to plant trees and shrubs, and to stay around long enough to see them grow. I wanted to create a proper perennial garden, as my father had before me. We were to go to Algiers for a two-year assignment, but before we left, we bought an old farm on the east side of Lake Cayuga in New York State. It was a wonderful place, with a big Victorian house, woods and fields sloping west toward the lake, a stream that ran into a hemlock-clad gorge, lots of waterfalls. As I stood behind the old farmhouse, I had a clear vision of a 250-foot flower border shimmering in refined yet radiant colors. But to keep reality in mind while we were in Algiers, I took snapshots of the area as it actually was: an unkempt strip of calf pasture and weedy no-man's-land, accented by a whirly clothes pole, a privy, a concrete outdoor fireplace painted red, a metal quonset hut, and a dilapidated shed.

The snapshots should have sobered me in Algiers as I pored over English gardening books (the American library had been dismantled),

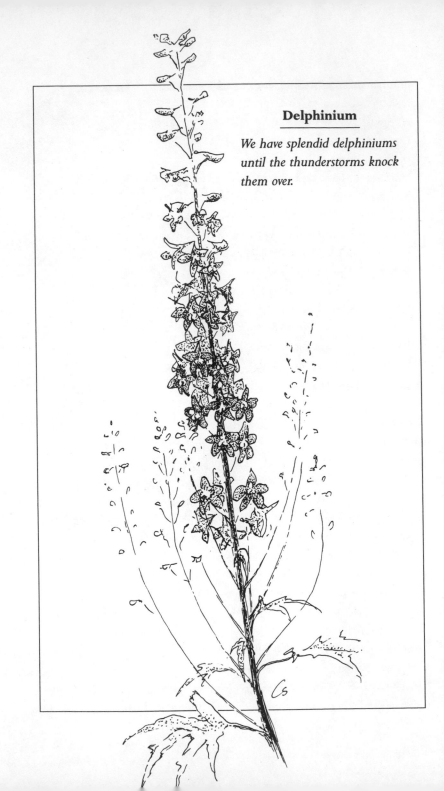

Delphinium

We have splendid delphiniums until the thunderstorms knock them over.

graph paper before me. But no—on I charged. I read about plants, their requirements, their growth habits and blooming times. I traced straight lines, swoops, and circles on my paper, establishing the locations of trees and shrubs, walks and walls. Finally, with delicious thrills of anticipation, I put in little blobs of color for the perennials.

I wanted a long stone wall to separate my flower border from my husband's vegetable garden and serve as a background for the flowers and shrubs. I drew the wall straight, to run east and west, parallel to the house and beyond. Then I played curves against it, cutting out openings to the vegetable garden. The little sassafras grove at the east end would be a woodland garden.

I selected trees and shrubs, both deciduous and evergreen, for I had read that one should use woody plants as well as flowers to make the garden attractive at all times of the year. (I didn't know then that I'd be ruining the appearance of the garden in winter by covering the tender plants with pine boughs, inverted bushel baskets, boxes, even old plastic garbage cans.)

I wrote to nurseries in the United States for catalogs. These materials gave me an idea of which plants would be available at home. Since at that time nursery catalogs didn't key their plants to U.S.D.A. hardiness zone maps, however, I got very little guidance from them as to which plants in the English books would be suitable for a garden in the Finger Lakes.

Luckily, having learned about the Gulf Stream in geography class, I had sense enough to know that although Great Britain is much farther north than New York State, the difference in climate is not what one might expect. It seems unfair, but there it is. All through my Algerian notes I find pathetic little entries such as "Ceonothus—gorgeous blue shrub. Hardy?" Then, often, a sad afterthought, "Prob. not." Nevertheless, I was able to get an indication of hardiness by learning the sources of some of the plants (Karakorum Mountains of Tibet, vicinity of Lake Baikal, Siberia) and by rejecting, regretfully, any plant the British cheerfully assured me could "tolerate a few degrees of frost."

I read Vita Sackville-West, Gertrude Jekyll, Edward Hyams, and Lanning Roper. I learned that colors should be subtly orchestrated, not just allowed to fight things out among themselves. I wrote down maxims of Hyams that I found in *An Englishman's Garden,* to wit:

> *Plants should not be allowed to count for more than their contribution to the total effect.*

and

> *The proper progression is from the whole to the parts, from the vistas to the details, which must be interesting.*

These rules I referred to whenever I felt myself getting out of hand.

One of the writers, knowing the gold-rush madness that is apt to hit the beginning gardener and cause the acquisitiveness that leads to chaos, or to overplanting at the least, says that if one sees a new plant and tries to think where to put it, rather than seeing a hole and trying to think what plant to put there, one is a plant collector, not a gardener.

When my husband's two-year stint in Algeria was up, I held an exhibition of my paintings—for I had been vigorously painting in Algeria as well as making garden plans—and sold enough to buy everything I needed to begin my garden. Soon I was back in New York, flailing away in earnest with a two-pronged Algerian mattock.

I could see immediately that one part of my plan had to be changed. The tool shed—along with the collapsed corncrib, many dead elms, a manure loader, and other assorted machinery—obstructed a view of the fields and lake that I hadn't realized was there. Instead of curving to a close around the shed, the border would have to sweep out into the view. That meant that I would have to forgo using the "theory of the unexpected," an idea I had been trying mentally and on paper to adapt to our terrain. The theory is that one should not be able to see all of a garden at once – that it is much more desirable to have a series of outdoor rooms, as it were, with garden opening into garden, and always something new and exciting ahead. In England it is done with yew or beech hedges, stone or brick walls. But with only me to do the work, I had not planned on a reproduction of the gardens at Sissinghurst, and faced with the geographical facts, I had to renounce that part of my plan in any case.

After reworking the plan, I translated the pencil lines on the graph paper into three-dimensional form by laying hose through the weeds, then rushing up to the roof to check on the design before driving in the stakes. Then I chopped down the weeds with a sickle and dug. I seemed to have chosen the site into which people had been pitching rocks and trash for at least a hundred years. But the soil, through desuetude, was more fertile than the land that had been farmed. (This was a secret observation; no announcements were made, lest they give birth to the idea of using the site for vegetables.)

I set about sawing the small dead elms and hauling them away, hoping to get help with the big obstacles as I went along. I was capable of removing rocks and trash, but there remained the sheds, privy, and quonset hut. Since my husband really wanted them to stay where they were, the removal operation took some time. After five years, the last of them disappeared.

But even George couldn't deal with the outdoor fireplace. Its concrete foundation resisted all the warlike implements with which I fell upon it. At length the chap who was digging our new septic system, having observed my mining operations and heard my wails of frustration, got behind the thing with his bulldozer and gently pushed it into a ravine.

To build a stone wall, one should dig down below the frost level and lay the stones properly. I found that after gathering them all from the surrounding fields and woods (with help from my husband and his tractor), it was about all I could do to lay them just under the surface of the soil. The plans stipulated that the wall be four feet high. It turned out to be two feet. Still, it took a lot of rocks, and I wouldn't like to build it again.

All the while I was reading gardening books, learning to propagate from seeds and cuttings, and studying plants in the gardens of the Cornell Plantations. I put in lawn, flower border, or wall, depending on the weather and the season.

I fetched many sacks of wood soil from the hemlock grove, taking a bit here and there so as not to deprive the trees; George would bring the sacks back on the wagon when he went down to get logs. The wood soil was for the woodland garden, where I planted most of the early-blooming things, including almost all the bulbs.

I dug steadily westward. George thought I wouldn't stop until I got to the lake, but stop I did, laying the last stone on the wall exactly six years from the time I had begun.

The English books I had studied were of great value to me as I designed the garden. Cornell and the New York State cooperative extension service were both extremely helpful, and I had access to books in both the public and the Cornell libraries. But even books don't keep one from making mistakes. It was difficult to plant things the correct distance apart, to visualize how big they would become, even when I knew the dimensions. Perhaps the problem was impatience. The big empty spaces made my spindly new plants look pathetic, so I put them too close together, purchasing present pleasure with future pain. I've learned not to do that, at least not with shrubs and trees.

Having lived for many years in countries around the Mediterranean, I have come to love the tough, moundy aromatic plants that cling to those dry stony hills: cistus, *Pistacia lentiscus,* myrtle, thyme, horehound, and even those prickly little kermes oak bushes *(Quercus coccifera)* that scratch the legs. Although cistus, which thrives in England, will not grow here, I have been able to give part of the border a Mediterranean look, I fancy, by using selections of helianthemum, thyme, santolina, lavender, and other dwarf shrubs. They do need protection from the winter winds and are the principal cause of the unsightly lumps in our winter garden. Yet they are worth the draw-backs for the joy they give the rest of the year.

Despite all precautions, it has taken me a long time to find out what plants will be happy here. I had to learn through experience that it isn't only the cold one has to worry about. I lost many a dear little alpine before I realized that although it would perch happily on my rocks at twenty degrees below zero, August would do it in. Neither water nor contrived shade will solace a soldanella at ninety-five degrees Fahrenheit. And in an area in which May often brings a week of ninety-degree-plus weather that wilts the rhododendron and primrose blossoms as they open, reducing them to limp rags, July and August are bound to bring the *coup de grâce* to any high alpine. The hot spell in May might easily be followed, I might add, by temperatures of twenty-eight degrees or lower. It's not only the extremes of temperature but also the manic-depressive behavior that do a lot of the damage. Add to that days of desiccating wind and glaring sun . . .

Besides the weather hazards, there is the problem of the non-vanishing wildlife—the deer, groundhogs, rabbits, chipmunks, squirrels, mice, and voles, all chewing ceaselessly, relentlessly at their different levels, from the high buds of the azaleas to the roots of the heather. I do what I can with hardware cloth, deer repellent, moth balls, orchard bait, and pine boughs. To protect the *enceinte* of our castle against the deer, George is slowly building an outer barrier, using multiflora roses and interwoven tree branches.

Amazing as it seems, however, there are hundreds of perennials that flourish here, bravely battling the weather and the fierce winds whipping in from the lake. There are masses and billows of species and cultivars of lavender, salvia, helianthemum, anemone, aquilegia, centranthus, and geranium. We have splendid delphiniums until the thunderstorms knock them over.

Among all of these the colors silver and gray are repeated, partly with artemisias of many kinds, so the garden is blues, whites, pinks, lavenders, and pale lemon yellows, with an occasional spot of crimson, woven together with silvery gray artemisia, veronica, santolina, and cerastium, and green-gray and blue-gray dianthus, nepeta, rue, aethionema, and lavender. Gray wafts even into the center of the heather and small-shrub section of the border, where the furry gray ears of *Stachys byzantina* and feathery artemisias end in an apotheosis of gray: a clump of tall, lavender-tipped Russian sage, *Perovskia atriplicifolia,* which makes a fountain of radiant, delicate silver.

Another of Hyam's maxims was that "one should confine oneself to placing discreet bursts of suitable color in a green landscape." He probably wouldn't approve of my garden in June, when the bursts of color obliterate the green landscape. But when I stand by the woods garden on a fine summer day and gaze at the borders moving in and out toward the west with the lake and the blue hills beyond, the whole scene looks almost as good as my original vision.

2

MASSES AND MULCHES

IN THIS COUNTRY, though a few citizens have, at one time or another, created notable gardens, the average citizen has been slow to interest himself in serious gardening–gardening for the joy of it, gardening as an art form. Even today, most advertisers and writers of garden books stress low maintenance. The idea seems to be how to impress your neighbors and improve the value of your property with the least possible effort. Gardening for *fun*–digging, designing, plant-ing, weeding, combining colors, learning about individual plants, satisfying their needs, discovering their special qualities–is an idea that has not really trickled through to our teeming masses. But now that some of us are beginning to perceive the possibilities of this stimulating, satisfying, and therapeutic pursuit, we are in some ways being hampered as well as helped by accepting every theory we encounter in English gardening books.

The garden literature to which we turn for instruction is largely British. Naturally: The British not only write (and write so well!) in a language we can read but have created marvelous gardens that we may easily learn from. Spanish and Italian gardens, superb as they may be, are of a different tradition in their design and conception and make use of plants that will not thrive in many parts of the United States. Oriental gardens do not always have the latter disadvantage, but since they are the product of a completely different philosophy and attitude toward nature and art, attempts to reproduce them in a Western country seem inappropriate to some of us.

When studying English garden books, we learn early on which plants cannot be grown in our difficult climates, but we may not think of discarding or tempering other ideas. There is, for example, the doctrine that plants must be marshaled in masses, each of its kind, in the flower garden or border. The Word is that everyone who is anyone designs his garden with groups of three, five, or seven but preferably nine or more plants (uneven numbers, always) set out as drifts, to use Miss Jekyll's word, but usually ending up as triangles.

Marrubium velutinum

The grayish foliage of the poppy consorted well with a felty marrubium, its neighbor, and was still giving much pleasure in October.

Now if one has a refined color sense and an estate garden with a four-hundred-foot border, large areas of the same color, rather than a spot here and there, will create a smashing effect. Masses of the same plant can even be repeated all down the border to achieve unity. It is indeed a sound idea, one that has contributed to the creation of some of the most glorious gardens in the world, in a country where climate, zeal, artistic sense, and the economic situation have combined favorably. (All of those elements are important, not least the economic situation.)

But most people have limited garden areas. Not only do they not have a border measuring four hundred by twenty-five feet, they may not even have a strip thirty feet long and five feet wide. To tell an ardent new gardener who possesses about fifty square feet of earth that he must plant only in masses is to break his heart and spirit—he wants to try many plants and plant combinations. Planting in large masses would so limit him that if he were to believe you, he would either lose his sense of adventure and settle for a few yews and hostas or give up gardening altogether.

Besides, when mass planting is combined with the new practice of mulching every plant (whether it likes it or not) with wood chips or some other weed-stifling substance in the interests of making a work-free garden, the little armies of plants standing at attention, each one surrounded by its allotment of mulch, have a most unnatural, regimented appearance. I've seen large gardens created on this plan that were tremendously impressive—great stout perennials and grasses shoulder to shoulder, all performing their duty, providing great blobs of yellow, great spikes of white, wide lakes of blue—impressive indeed and good in a public park, but not charming, not appealing, not endearing, and not terribly interesting. Imagine instead a garden that is composed of both groups and individuals, where the plants are not each encircled by wood chips, where they are growing chummily together, where they may even be leaning on or twining through or over one another. Unexpected things happen as a traveling geranium pokes its pink blossoms up into a gaura, suddenly bringing out the pink of the gaura's calyces. A poppy mallow may unfold its crimson-magenta cup over a little patch of 'Silver Carpet' lamb's ears – a combination so good the gardener wonders why he hadn't planned it.

Last summer something died in the front of one of my border curves, making a choice spot available. I turned a *Papaver anomalum* out of its pot and poked it in, where it proceeded to expand, grateful to be out of the pot, and put forth one silky white cup after another. The grayish foliage of the poppy consorted well with a felty marrubium, its neighbor, and was still giving much pleasure in October. I don't wish I had three, five, seven, or nine white poppies in that spot. Having just the one concentrates the viewer's attention on every aspect of stem, leaf, bud, and flower. For the sake of repetition of theme, I've planted a few others here and there down the front of the border. That's it, you see. Harmony is the main thing, and harmony can be achieved by repetition of color, shape, and texture. You can plant a group of blue Siberian iris, say, then a single pink cranesbill, which will make a substantial mass all by itself, and a gray santolina. You can then let a low-spreading rose ('The Fairy', perhaps) repeat the pink of the geranium, and let one billowy *Geranium magnificum* pick up the blue of the iris, and so on. You might have three or five columbines together – they are so airy-fairy that they do better in groups – but you don't need masses of plants that make an impact singly.

Some stately plants, such as dictamnus, really should stand in splendid isolation and not have their individuality swamped by surrounding siblings. This everyone admits.

Finally, perennials that go dormant in mid- or late season should never be planted in numbers, as the gap left when they disappear is too large to be covered by any device I know of, and I've tried a few. Someone recently suggested in a magazine article that five bleeding hearts should be planted together in a perennial border. Since each one would be about as big as a bushel basket in a few years' time, I wondered how the writer proposed to fill the space for July, August, and September.

I couldn't resist, several years ago, planting together three Oriental poppies of pale, medium, and dark smoky lavender. For the brief interval when they are blooming, I feast my eyes on them as greedily as I can, for I know that in a few weeks I'll be trying yet another scheme to cover what looks like an empty stadium in the middle of the border. Annuals never seem to get going in time to do the job, and perennials planted in close are too discouraged to carry on after having been leaned on by the poppies. The last couple of years I've shamelessly stood two huge potted plants *(Convulvulus cneorum* and *Myrtus communis)* in the crucial spots. Some people don't even notice I'm cheating.

3

LAVENDER

. . . to perfume linnen, apparell, gloves and leather and the dryed flowers to comfort, and dry up the moisture of a cold braine . . .

—*John Parkinson*

LAVENDERS ARE IN A SAD state of confusion. Pity the poor horticulturist or amateur botanist who winds his way through *Hortus Third* and the countless works of herbal authorities. He will end up with his head spinning when he discovers that *Lavandula spica* is the same as *L. angustifolia,* that *Lavandula vera* is *L. angustifolia* subsp. *angustifolia* and is also sometimes called *L. officinalis,* that *Lavandula intermedia* (*Lavandin* or "French lavender") is a cross between *L. angustifolia* and *L. latifolia* ("Spike lavender"). But *L. stoechas* is also called "French lavender." And what is Dutch lavender?

Henry Head of Norfolk Lavender Ltd., England, tried in the *Herbal Review* of 1982 to clear up the question of what is "English lavender":

> L. angustifolia angustifolia *has been described as* L. officinalis, L. vera, L. spica *(not to be confused with spike laven-*

Lavender

The plant has long been grown around beehives . . . its honey being much prized . . .

der), French lavender, Dutch lavender, True lavender and English lavender, and I have heard Stoechas called French
lavender and Dutch lavender.

It is my view therefore that English lavender can only be
lavender that has been grown in England, French lavender in
France, and so on.

Best leave it all to the professional botanists. Perhaps the rest of us
need only know that of the twenty-eight species of lavender, most of
them coming from the Mediterranean regions, only five or six species
and their cultivars are used in our gardens, and of these only *L. spica
(angustifolia)* and *L. vera (angustifolia angustifolia)* or their cultivars are
hardy in the north. After that the only confusion we face is the
nomenclature of the cultivars. The authorities describe *L.* 'Munstead'
and *L.* 'Twickel Purple' as having "dark aster-violet" blossoms, but the
plants that are being sold under those names by the nurseries I deal
with have pale lavender blossoms. Only *L.* 'Hidcote' has dark spikes.
Pink- and white-flowered varieties are also in a state of indecision. But
given the embarrassing fact that the Royal Horticultural Society gave
an Award of Merit to *Lavandula angustifolia* 'Nana Atropurpurea', not
knowing it was actually *Lavandula angustifolia* 'Hidcote', and later
"highly commended" *L.a.* 'Nana Alba', which was really *L.a.* 'Alba',
how can we, the uninitiated, hope to fathom these many mysteries?

Apparently, part of the confusion is due to cultivars' having been
developed at different nurseries from the same parents, so that the
resulting offspring, although bearing different names, are almost identical. Also, some nurserymen have been offering plants grown from
seed of cultivars, only a percentage of which can be expected to come
true. *L.* 'Hidcote' comes truer than most, but solely by vegetative
propagation can one be sure of getting a legitimate child of a cultivar.

Be that as it may, lavender of any parentage is a pure delight for all
of us who adore its gray foliage and its fresh fragrance and value it
dried for scenting our houses in winter.

People have loved lavender for a long time. It was valued by the Egyptians, Phoenicians, Greeks, and Romans. The Romans substituted it for the expensive nard they got from India to perfume their baths—we are fairly certain, at least, that their "false nard" was lavender. The name is thought to derive from the Latin verb *lavare*, to wash (*launder* comes from the same word).

In southern Europe lavender was grown in monastery gardens during the twelfth century. In the thirteenth century a Welsh physician refers to it in a list of medicinal plants as a dry powdered drug imported from southern countries. We know that by the next century Emperor Charles VI of France was lolling about on satin cushions stuffed with lavender and that courtiers in England in Chaucer's time had access to it. Around the time of Queen Elizabeth (who liked lavender jelly with roast lamb), it became the property of common mortals, having been found to be hardy in northern Europe.

Lavender has been put to countless practical uses. The volatile oil, found mostly in the plant's extremities—bracts, corollas, and calyces (the flowers contain much more oil than the stems and leaves)—is combined with alcohol to make lavender water. For centuries oil from both the flowers (lavender oil) and the whole plant (oil of spike) has been used by painters as a vehicle for pigments. The plant has long been grown around beehives, along with thyme, marjoram, and rosemary, its honey being much prized, as is that of all aromatic plants.

In the first century A.D., when Dioscorides was writing, *L. stoechas* was used for strengthening drinks, as a tranquilizing ointment, and in antipoison pills (one wouldn't like to have to depend on it for that). It was also used in baths to alleviate symptoms of nervous disorders. The Egyptians found it salutary for eye diseases, and it has been resorted to for uterine disorders, for coughs, for fainting fits, as a digestive aid, and as an ingredient in palsy drops. Old herbals recommend lavender for "light migrain" and "simmering of the braine". (Now we know where to lay our heads when the going gets rough.) In one French document, dated 1826, I found the following:

Lavender is in great demand, especially in the higher classes of society, for daily toilet applications. . . . It is also an agreeable and available remedy for . . . headaches and other slight maladies to which persons of gentle breeding are subjected. *

Those were the days when upper-class people were considered to be of such superior stuff that even their illnesses were not the same as those of the lower orders.

The most widely grown lavenders today are small, one- to three-foot June-flowering shrubs with narrow green-gray leaves. The labiate, usually lavender blossoms are borne on numerous square-stemmed stalks that rise straight from the shrubs, the small flowers circling the spikes, six to ten in each circle, widely placed at the bottom, close-packed at the top.

The various species of lavender have slightly different odors: *L. stoechas* contains more camphor than other lavenders, so it is used in ointments, liniments, and moth repellents, as well as in sachets and perfume. The oil from *L. spica* is used largely in soaps and perfumes, and the oil of *L. vera* is put into soft drinks, ice cream, candy, and baked goods as a flavoring, as well as for scent in perfume.

Both England and France specialize in lavender and its products, which seems odd given their different climates. *Lavender spica* will grow as far north as Sweden if it is properly situated and is given winter protection, but its fragrance will not equal that of the same plant grown in a hot, dry environment. This I know from experience, as one of my daughters sent me a little sachet she made while staying in the Vaucluse District in France. I had to admit that the scent was greatly superior to that of my own beloved lavender.

---

*Baron Frederic de Gingins-Lassarez, *Histoire naturelle des lavandes.* Paris: Charles Béchet, 1826. Translated and reprinted by the New England Unit of the Herb Society of America, Boston 1967.

The aroma of lavender grown in rich or damp soil will be much less pleasant than that of plants grown in spare, dry soil. In richer soil the plants grow bigger but have less fragrance, since they don't produce as much volatile oil. On very damp soil the plants blacken and die.

One is told that lavender needs to be protected from the wind in winter, but I've found that to be simply not true. It seems to prefer a free circulation of air to being cuddled and cossetted. The secret to growing lavender, I believe, is to give it gritty, limy soil with perfect drainage and all the sun your region has to offer. I have it growing in ordinary soil on level ground in the perennial border, where I occasionally lose a plant or branches of plants. However, in a raised stone bed where it has next to no nourishment and is lashed fiercely by every winter wind that blows, no piece of it has ever died, and it self-seeds so lavishly that it is threatening to take over the whole bed. This small raised bed is built around the stump of an old elm tree. New lavender plants are now growing not only between the layers of rock but even out of the old dry stump, where no soil is visible at all. I do lay pine boughs over the plants where I can, but the winter gales send them flying across the lawn, so the lavenders are usually uncovered. It must be that lavender, being a resinous plant like the pine, can resist cold very well if it is not waterlogged. Both rich soil and moisture, apparently, not only keep the plant from producing its quota of volatile oil, they also make it more susceptible to winter kill.

One problem with lavender is its appearance in spring, especially those plants growing on level ground. One cuts off the scraggly branches and trims the others back to where new buds are emerging, but still it looks so disheveled, one wants to apologize for it to early garden visitors. In benign climates lavender is often used as hedge material for herb gardens, but it should not be considered for this assignment north of zone 6, since a hedge should look neat at all times.

Now here is an example of what is perhaps our national horticultural paranoia, that everything grows better in English gardens. I had thought that in England, lavender always looked splendid—after all, the English practically invented it, never mind that it comes from the Mediterranean. One famous English garden writer even includes it in her list of plants that have "contented-looking foliage all the year round." So imagine my glee when I found it castigated in another distinguished English garden book for its scruffy appearance "nine months of the year." According to the writer, it looks forlorn from early August, when its flowers are finished, until the following May, when it puts forth new growth. Lavender, he says, "is one of our most cherished eyesores." Well, thought I with great satisfaction, it doesn't look bad *here* for nine months. In fact, it often flowers a second time in late summer if it has been sheared in time. It even looks good in late October. Since in the Northeast we hardly see our gardens from November through March (if they are not covered with snow, they are covered with pine boughs), we can hardly hold those five months of eclipse against the lavender. It's only in April and May that we feel it could manage better if it tried harder. And that makes seven months, not nine.

Still . . . the English can grow *Lavender stoechas*, that neat little piney thing with flying purple bracts on top of each spike, and the nearly white-foliaged *L. lanata*. I envy them that. They can probably leave the ferny pinnate *Lavenders multifida* and *dentata* out-of-doors, too, whereas we must bring them inside.

The lavenders in my garden are mostly old bushes of *L. vera*, grown from seed years ago, and lavenders I have bought as 'Munstead', 'Twickel Purple', and 'Hidcote' and their descendents. There is also one murky whitish-pink lavender called 'Jean Davis'. I don't recommend it. The 'Twickel Purple' and 'Munstead' both bear pale lilac-colored flowers, the only difference between the plants being that the 'Munstead' is perhaps a bit more compact. 'Hidcote' is by far the best, having the grayest foliage and the deepest purple flowers. The only other cultivars that seem to be offered by nurseries in the United States are *L.* 'Grey Lady' and *L.a.* 'Dwarf Blue'.

The lavenders on the rock wall are growing with aubrietias,

pasque flowers, creeping gypsophilas, and other rock garden plants. Other lavenders are found toward the front of the perennial border, among the helianthemums, santolinas, dianthus, armerias, nepetas, and thymes, all of which enjoy similar treatment: lime, spare soil, not very much water, no fertilizer. They look very cheery and compatible – Mediterranean, actually, making mounds and tussocks like the plants on those tufa-rocky hills.

If you have lavender but would like to have more without expense, consider taking cuttings. This can be done in either spring or fall. Prepare a rooting bed in the ground or in a large flat or pot by mixing a lot of sharp sand or fine grit with peat. Dampen it thoroughly and press it down. Take three- to six-inch shoots that have neither flowered nor been *thinking* of flowering from a vigorous young plant, preferably a two-year-old. As with dianthus or any other plant you are trying to root, remove the lower leaves neatly with a sharp tool, dip the cuttings in water, then in rooting compound, and press them firmly into holes made with the blunt end of a pencil. Each cutting should touch the bottom of its hole. Experts will tell you to envelop your pot or flat in a plastic bag, but whenever I've tried that, my cuttings have mildewed – and gray plants are especially prone to mildew when their air supply is cut off. I root cuttings of all kinds in a sand–peat mixture under a wisteria bush, where they get light but no sun, and cover them with jars or cloches. When I'm dealing with lavender cuttings, I prop the cloches up a bit with a stick so that fresh air can still enter the chamber.

Cuttings taken in late spring should be of a size to pot by late summer. But in the north it seems wiser to winter them in a sunny window indoors and plant them the following May, or put them in a cold frame. If you take cuttings in August or September, you can leave them in the ground, with their covers firmly in place, until May. If they are in a pot or flat, of course, you can bring it inside and pot up the plants when they are ready. A cutting is usually ready to lift when it shows new growth at the top.

Another way of propagating lavender, says the garden encyclopedia, is by careful division in spring when the new leaf buds appear or directly after they have been shorn of their blossom stems in summer. The word *careful* intimidates me, and I have never tried it. One is told to lift, pull apart, and replant the sections that have many small rootlets at the base of the stem. The tops should be trimmed to balance the amount of root the section is carrying. Protecting the new divisions with pine boughs for several days to a week helps keep them from dehydrating until their roots resume operations.

You must have patience if you attempt to raise lavender plants from seed. The seeds are decidedly stubborn, usually waiting for a month or more before making a move. Sometimes they don't move at all. At other times dozens of little plants will appear as if there were nothing to it. Then you must be careful not to water them too much or they will all fall flat on their faces from damp-off. If you have planted them in a spare, sandy, sterile mixture in a sterile flat or pot, you will have taken the proper precautions. After that, water them only when you think they must be desperate for a drink.

That fine herbarist Gertrude Foster says that some of the best seedlings come from seed that has been allowed to ripen on the plants, then scattered whole (without being rubbed out of the seed heads) on a prepared seed bed and left to winter out-of-doors. If one is planting into a flat, with one's own or purchased seed, she says, decorticated seed should be sown on half an inch of sand that has been sifted over potting soil. Do not use sphagnum moss or vermiculite, as it stays too wet for lavender.

If your new seed-grown plants are still only a few inches tall by fall, they will need protection in the form of salt hay or pine boughs or perhaps even cloches, or they may spend their first winter indoors or in a cold frame.

One of the reasons for growing lavender is to be able to harvest and dry it for winter fragrance in the house. It is wonderful for the purpose, retaining its scent for many months, even years. My problem is that I cannot bear to cut it off just as it's coming into bloom or shortly after, as directed. Its contribution to the general effect of the garden is so valuable that I usually don't cut it back until it has finished blooming and is about to set seed. If I cut it then, I usually get a second flowering and am able to harvest seed for the following year from that late crop. But of course, there is no lavender-stuffed pillow on which to lay a simmering braine.

If you are stronger-minded than I, be sure you cut your lavender at the proper time, when the flowers on the top of the stalk are open and the bottom ones are at least showing color. Either hang it in bunches upside down in a dark airy place or, if you have trimmed off leaves with the stalks of blossoms, lay it all on a screen in the same dark, airy place. When the stems are dry enough to snap in two easily, you can strip off the flowers to use in potpourri, saving the stems to put in containers under the couch. You may prefer to use the flowers still on their stems in dried bouquets or other winter arrangements.

Like Dr. Spock in his baby book, I have left discussing afflictions until the last. (I always appreciated that when I was growing children instead of plants; no sense in scaring anyone.) There is a lavender disease with the wonderful name of *shab*. *Lavandula phoma* is its formal name. The symptoms are withering and death of young shoots in May or June. Later the disease extends downward to older parts of the plant. Look at the young withered shoots under a magnifying glass. If you see small black dots, that's it – they are the spore-producing capsules of the fungus. Seize the plant forthwith, uproot and burn it.

4

WHO SHOULD DESIGN YOUR GARDEN?

IN A BOOK by one of our doyennes of horticulture, I once read that no property owner should design his or her own garden but should engage the services of a licensed landscape architect—a garden designer, that is. She could always tell at a glance, she said, whether the job had been done by a professional or by the amateur-owner himself. So can I, I dare say, but we differ in that I usually prefer the work of the latter. And for the reasons that follow.

An alarming homogenization of gardens is taking place in this country, the result of an American tendency that seems to be stronger than we are. We get onto an idea and diffuse it by the many media at our disposal. Everyone is eager to go along with the latest. People buy it, take lessons in it, read it, eat it, or build it. Right now gardening is *in,* thank goodness. We are finally beginning to be interested in growing plants and beautifying our surroundings. New nurseries are sprouting, the cooperative extension agency is sponsoring master gardener courses, and universities are offering more courses in horti-

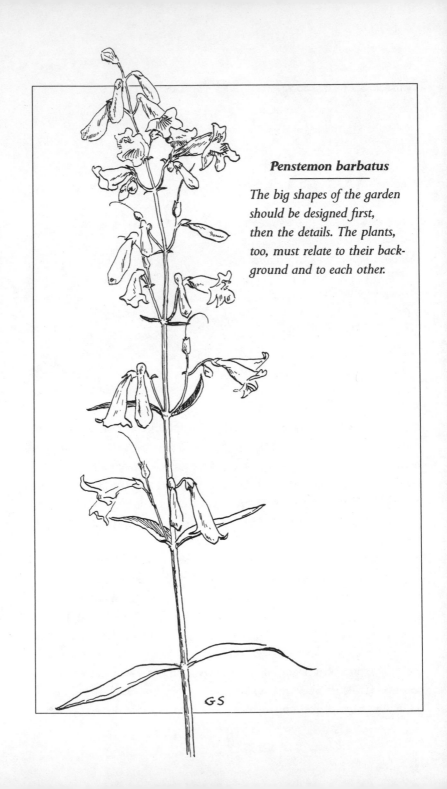

Penstemon barbatus

The big shapes of the garden should be designed first, then the details. The plants, too, must relate to their background and to each other.

culture and landscape design. All of this is good news, but our fatal tendency is already becoming visible in the gardens that are being designed or redesigned–they are beginning to look almost interchangeable. There is a deadly Landscape Architect touch that is all too visible, the touch of people who speak of dealing with "plant material"–a blood-curdling term. Stone walls, railway ties, and thick wood-chip mulches are much in evidence. The latest in plant material is rounded up and put to use: the newest grasses, the latest hostas, the last word in daylilies, ferns, and cultivars of *Rhododendron yakushimanum.* Soon you'll be able to pick up a garden in Chicago and put it down in Boston without anyone's knowing the difference.

We do need to train people in garden design, but we must make sure that the trainees learn about plants as well as design. They must also realize that every garden is ideally the work of one person, the result of his sensitive reaction to a particular area, so that it may be enhanced rather than blighted by the imposition of a preconceived idea. And I am not the first to say it's just as important to learn what to let alone as what to change. As each spot on earth is unique, so should each garden be unique.

If a property owner wants his place landscaped, redesigned, or made into a garden and feels incapable of working out a plan himself, he should find an expert whose views are compatible with his own, and they should work closely together. This way he will not deprive himself of his share of pride in and enjoyment of the results. We can only appreciate to a degree work that is done for us but in which we haven't participated, as Jane Loudon pointed out when she was urging women to work in their own gardens. Mrs. Loudon, the first professional woman horticulturist, whose book *Gardening for Ladies* appeared in England in 1840, wrote,

The great point is to exercise our own skill and ingenuity, for we all feel so much more interested in what we do ourselves than in what is done for us, that no [one] is likely to become

fond of gardening who does not do a great deal with [his] own hands. *

If one loves plants and the activity of gardening but has had no training in garden (or any other kind of) design, one can educate oneself. The libraries are full of garden design books, and graph paper is available at the paper store. Plot the property, putting in the existing features, no matter how crudely–buildings, trees, walkways. Then make a plan that will harmonize with the lines and shapes already there. Oddly enough, if it looks good on paper, it will look good when you construct it. When people are dissatisfied with what they have wrought in their gardens, it is usually because they have worked at the thing piecemeal, sometimes over a period of years, sticking a tree here, a perennial garden there, never considering the property as a whole. Every shrub you plant, every path you trace, every flower bed you lay out relates to what is already there. You can achieve harmony only by repetition of theme. If your driveway curves, try to repeat that curve somewhere–in the shape of a flower bed, hedge, or pool. Your house is built on straight lines? Repeat those lines, at least in paths or edges of beds close to the house. If you're building raised beds, employ a material that is already in use in the immediate area; if the house is of wood, you might use wood or railway ties instead of brick and vice versa for raised beds near a brick house. If there is a strong line of hedge, think where you might repeat the theme. Repetition of vertical lines is just as helpful as repetition of horizontal ones. Work with the straight trunks of young trees, lines of a fence, the strong vertical blades of Japanese iris, even of tall grasses if they seem to be suitable for your garden. (I myself prefer to see them used in wide

---

* Loudon, Jane, *Ladies Companion to the Flower Garden (Gardening for Ladies* and *The Flower Garden),* edited by A.J. Downing. New York: John Wiley, 1863.

open spaces with lots of wind and air around them.) Repeat colors of flowers and foliage.

The big shapes of the garden should be designed first, then the details. The plants, too, must relate to their background and to each other. Nothing has value except what its environment gives it. A flame-red azalea looks tawdry against a brick building but glorious against dark trees.

In plumping for homemade gardens I must admit my intolerance of other people's ideas on what constitutes a proper garden. That it's homemade doesn't cause me to temper my cries of pain at the sight of raised beds made of cement blocks, of planted tires, of top-heavy, overfed and overbred dahlias lashed, like felons, to rows of stakes, of marigolds marching around a fake wishing well, of large circles of flaming cannas edged with mournful wax begonias in the middle of a pocket-handkerchief lawn, or squares of celosia in unlikely colors and textures, sharing the assignment of afflicting the eye with plastic figures of gnomes, deer, poultry, or those damned ubiquitous pink flamingos. Theoretically, I want people who like petunias planted in wringer washing machines to *have* them. I want people to create, around their houses, plantings and arrangements that satisfy *their* sense of beauty, and I'm glad that they have the impulse to create anything nonutilitarian at all. *De gustibus non est disputandum,* I proclaim of such gardeners—but still, I hope they don't move in next door.

5

ALMOST ALL
ABOUT WINDFLOWERS

IT'S EASY TO FALL IN LOVE with anemones. In trying to analyze their appeal I come up with the words "guileless," "pure," "innocent," and "elegant."

The flowers that inspire those adjectives are members of the buttercup family, or Ranunculaceae. They have compound dissected or divided leaves, and their flowers have not petals but showy sepals that we take for petals. Their many stamens, sometimes surrounding a central green knob, are part of their attraction, particularly when the flower is white. Their native habitats, almost all in the north temperate zone, include alpine peaks, dry grassy Mediterranean hillsides, and dense shady woods. Some anemones need limy grit to flourish, others want rich moist soil. They range in size from a few inches high to four feet. One group is tuberous-rooted, others are rhizomatous. Different species flower in spring, summer, and fall. At least twenty species are found in North America alone, including two pulsatillas.

Which brings us to an area in which the taxonomists are divided. Some of those who give out the word, such as the writers of *Hortus*

Anemone hybrida

. . . *stunning tall, late-blooming perennials bearing elegant
buds and then flowers of
white, pale pink, rose, or
plum from late August into
October.*

Third, list pulsatillas under anemones. The European pasqueflower, called *Pulsatilla vulgaris* in Harkness's *Seedlist Handbook* as well as most rock garden books and the Royal Horticultural Society's *Dictionary of Gardening,* is *Anemone pulsatilla* in *Hortus.* What many other authorities refer to as *Pulsatilla alpina, Hortus* calls *"Anemone alpina (Pulsatilla alpina),"* and so on. I'm telling you this so that if you can't find a particular anemone in a garden book, you should look under both the *a*'s and the *p*'s.

There are several basic differences between the pulsatillas and other anemones, but the one most readily noticed by gardeners is the way they form their seeds. In pulsatillas each flat seed in its thin container is attached to a style, or part of the pistil, that eventually becomes feathery. A pulsatilla flower gone to seed carries a spherical, fluffy gray ball, similar to the seed cluster of clematis, which gradually loosens and releases each feathery style to fly off with its seed. This method of self-propagation contrasts with that of many other anemones whose spent flowers form what looks like a thimble—a dotted, dense, truncated cone. These cones, as the seed matures, expand and set adrift little wads of cotton in which the seeds are swathed. Four of the American anemones, *A. virginiana, caroliniana, riparia,* and *cylindrica,* are called thimbleweed because they are of this group.

Pulsatillas are held dear by many people partly because they bloom so early in the spring. The best known and most widely planted of this group is the pasqueflower, or Easter flower *(P. vulgaris),* which does indeed often bloom at Easter time, even in northern North America. Right now, although it is only the middle of March, pasqueflowers on my wall are making preparations to bloom. In the center of the dry brown lace of last year's foliage small pointed furry ears are poking up, their rose-colored rounded bases just showing. Soon each plant will look like a nest of gray rabbits, and the lavender or wine-colored cups, formed of satiny sepals, will begin to open in the nest, their stems growing taller each day until they reach ten or twelve inches. Plants that are pleased with their situation will carry more than forty blossoms at a time and will seed themselves into the most unpromising sites they can find—rocky, sandy, or woody places, wherever there is almost no nourishment. There they will thrive if the soil is sweet, if no moisture remains long on their roots, if they are baked by the sun and whipped by the wind. There are several cultivars of pasqueflower in white, purple, and red, the last, 'Rubra,' sometimes coming in a beautiful claret. They are variable when grown from seed.

Many other pulsatillas (or anemones of the pulsatilla group) are natives of Europe and Asia. Of the two from America, *Anemone* or *Pulsatilla patens nuttaliana (hirsutissima)*, which grows in the West, is similar to the pasqueflower, holding its glistening lavender cups clothed in silver fur close to the ground before the foliage unfurls. The mound reaches about six inches. Other forms of *A.* or *P. patens* are found in Europe and Asia.

One of the most enticing descriptions of a plant I've ever read was Reginald Farrer's passage on *Anemone (Pulsatilla) vernalis:*

> *Anemone vernalis* takes us high high into the Alps. . . .
> Spread out flat upon the ground, still sere and bare with
> the passing of winter, lie pressed the two or three carrotty
> leaves, more coarsely and sparingly cut than in any [other]
> Pulsatilla; next, an inch or two of stem, shaggy with fur of
> bronzy gold, a fluffy frill of the same, and then, almost
> sitting upon the moor, like some mystic water-lily, a great
> goblet-shaped flower, staring up to the sun, white as an
> opalescent pearl within, and tasselled with fire, while the
> outside of the pearl is ashimmer with gold and violet silk,
> iridescent as it catches the sun in countless shifting shades
> of lilac and fawn and milk . . .*

It almost brings tears of longing to one's eyes. Two years ago I

---

*Farrer, Reginald, *My Rock Garden*. Pawlet, Vermont: Theophrastus, 1971 (1907).

actually germinated seed of this alpine goddess and set the plants out in a raised bed. I failed to incorporate grit and lime into the soil, so for that reason or because of our nonalpine climate, the plants produced only a few rather muddy and undistinguished blossoms last spring. I mean to transplant them and go on trying for something that might approach, however distantly, the sublimity of what Farrer saw on the mountain. I'd like to try *A.* or *P. alpina,* too, if I can find it in a seed exchange list. It grows taller than the six-inch *vernalis,* to as high as eighteen inches, and has white flowers with blue on the reverse side. There's an *alpina sulphurea* as well.

As for the proper anemones, over which there is no argument, most people are familiar with the ones that are sold by bulb companies, who supply the tubers. Unfortunately, the bulb dealers often fail to inform gardeners that most of them – 'St. Brigid', 'St. Bavo', and 'De Caen' – are not hardy in cold climates. They come from the species *A. coronaria* and *A. pavonina* and are often referred to as florists' anemones. One sees great glorious bunches of them on all the street corners of Europe in the spring. The scarlet windflower, *A. fulgens,* is listed for zone 5 in one catalog. Since it is a cross between *A. pavonina* and *A. hortensis* and since each spring *A. pavonina* clothes the brown hills of Turkey with cups of pink, lavender, and scarlet, I would be overjoyed to be able to grow it here, at least the red one, in memory of happy years.

Another tuberous anemone, *A. appenina,* is too tender for the North, but *A. blanda,* from Europe and Asia Minor, has the same daisylike blossoms as *appenina,* and it survives and spreads. *Appenina* is usually offered only in blue (the so-called blue of catalog copy, that is), but *blanda* is to be had in pink and white as well. I have *A.b.* 'White Splendor' and 'Blue Star' in light humusy soil on the edge of the woods garden, where they are somewhat protected by surrounding trees and shrubs. Nevertheless, I cover them with pine boughs in late fall, just to make sure. They start to shine through the boughs in very early spring, and when I carefully lift off the branches, I see hundreds of polished shoots, each year more numerous than the year before.

'White Splendor' is larger and more dramatic than the blue but doesn't spread with such generosity. 'Blue Stars' are beginning to be sprinkled all over that area of the garden.

The same can be said of another daisylike six-inch plant, the European wood anemone *A. nemorosa.* I have sent to Oregon for cultivars, *A.n. robinsoniana* and 'Allenii', only to have them die or fail to multiply, whereas one that came as a bonus in a gift clump of Japanese painted fern, is turning up everywhere. In the wild it varies considerably; hunting for special forms and colors has long been a favorite activity of English gardeners. *A. nemorosa* sends slender stems up from small twiggy rhizomes. The leaves are three parted and deeply cleft—extremely pretty.

The American wood anemone, *A. quinquefolia,* is not quite so charming as the European one, but it has a delicate appeal all its own, with its single small white flowers swaying on fragile stems above the three deeply cut involucral leaves. It grows where the soil is acid, rich, and always moist. *A. canadensis,* another native of our woods, is a tougher individual and will ramp all over your woods if given a fair start. It will take full sun as well as shade, so more areas are available in which it can spread its thin, brown, ever-multiplying roots. It will fling its gleaming white blossoms up as high as two feet above the palmately divided buttercup foliage. If it is growing in good moist loamy soil it may flower from May to September.

Some people consider *Anemone deltoidea* the best of the American wood anemones—as fine as the European *nemorosa.* It should be planted in rich humus in a woodland area where its running roots can move about easily. The low, much-divided, shiny dark green leaves will be enhanced by the appearance on six-inch stems of two-inch white blossoms, sometimes with a hint of pink or blue. This anemone comes from the evergreen forests of the west.

A yellow wood anemone from Europe and Siberia, *A. ranunculoides,* is short and tuberous rooted, with three- to five-part, deeply cut leaves and golden-yellow single or semidouble flowers. You can often get seed for this from seed exchanges and use your plants in shady or partly shady sections of the garden. In Alan Bloom's *Alpines for your Garden* there is a dazzling picture of it.

For years I've been trying to germinate seed of a tall (eighteen-inch) anemone—*A. narcissiflora*—that carries its pinkish white flowers in umbels. It comes from the moist meadows of mountains in Europe and Asia and looks wonderful in pictures but will have nothing to say to me. With fresh seed it might be a different story.

I do have three potted plants of *Anemone rupicola* out in the cold frame, raised from seed last year. We will see this spring whether they will accept being this far from the Himalayas and will produce their large white flowers. They are said to be lovely, with pink undersides. I must get the plants out of the cold frame soon and into "rich, well-drained soil in partial shade," as my instructions direct.

There are dozens of pots of *A. magellanica* in the nursery. It's a favorite of mine, appealing in a quiet way. It holds its many eight-inch stems straight up above the divided foliage, and when they are all almost exactly the same height, each one pops out a small, flat, cream-colored flower. These subsequently make thimbles of cotton-covered seed. So do the big robust anemones *multifida* and *crinita*, which are similar to *magellanica* but larger, including their off-white flowers. That is, the plants I raised from seed are off-white; *Hortus* doesn't list *crinita* but says the flowers of *multifida*, which comes from our western states and Alaska, can be white or yellowish.

The descriptions of *Anemone palmata* puzzle me—they don't quite tally with the appearance of some plants that hatched out here from seed so labeled. They say it is nine inches high with two-inch golden or yellow flowers. Mine are yellowish cream. Extremely handsome plants but possibly not *palmata*? You can't ever be sure with seed exchange seed.

Of *Anemone sylvestris* I am sure, and sure, too, that it must be the prettiest of all the medium-height white anemones. A delightful refined yet ebullient creature, it gives freely of its pure white fragrant blossoms for many weeks in spring and often again in fall. The buds nod like those of poppies, then straighten up to display their goldenstamened flowers to best advantage. Its stolons are busy underground and the clumps keep spreading, yet the plant could never be called aggressive. One is told to place it in woods soil in shade, so that is where I obediently put it, but my neighbor has a great thrifty clump of it baking on a sunny bank where it couldn't look healthier.

Wayside offers an eighteen-inch *Anemone lesseri,* with flowers of "rich rosy carmine" that appear in early summer. Wayside and others say it's a *multifida* × *sylvestris* hybrid, but how can a white and a "white or yellowish" (see *Hortus Third, A. multifida*) flower produce a red one? *Hortus* doesn't list it, but the *RHS Dictionary of Gardening* says the flowers of *A. lesseri* can be white, yellow, purplish, or *rose.* The same dictionary's notes on *A. multifida* describe this American native as bearing greenish, whitish, yellow, or *red* flowers. That explains how *A. lesseri* can be red, but who can explain why our *Hortus* can't describe our plant as thoroughly as the *RHS Dictionary?* I have pots of *A. lesseri* whose blossoming I await with impatience. Will they be "rich rosy carmine" or purplish, yellow, or white? Presumably the rose form is being propagated vegetatively by Wayside, but since my plants come from seed, I can't be sure of their color.

We have taken the long way round for any reader who was looking for a discussion and perhaps a clarification of the "Japanese" anemone situation. Let me state firmly that I have no intention of trying to untangle a skein that my betters have failed to untangle. I'd thought, until I went into the subject seriously, that there were *A. japonica, A. hupehensis,* and *A. vitifolia* species, and then hybrids or special forms of these. So much may be true, but I know for sure only that the white *A. vitifolia* species exists, for I raised it from seed (not hardy, unfortunately). As for the others, plants from seed labeled *Anemone hupehensis* proved to be indistinguishable from plants I purchased as *A. japonica,* and after poring over many books, I can only conclude that these anemones have been hopelessly jumbled. *A. vitifolia robustissima* is easy—it's a pale pink, two- to four-foot anemone that resembles the other tall fall-blooming ones except that it blooms a month earlier. The other ones, whether sold as *A. japonica* or *hupehensis* or *hupehensis japonica* or *A. hybrida,* are all stunning tall, late-blooming perennials bearing elegant buds and then flowers of white, pale pink, rose, or plum from late August into October. The singles resemble dogwood blossoms. Since the plants have long woody taproots, they are notoriously difficult to move. They also have very lively and enterprising horizontal underground stolons, so once they hit their stride, they'll walk all over your garden. I've recently dug out, or tried to dig out, all the ones I've acquired as species (although now I know the classification is not so simple as that) and replaced them with cultivars with demure names like 'Alice', 'Queen Charlotte', and 'Margarette', feeling that individuals so named could hardly prove to be louts and bullies. I am sanguine but not certain and will report later.

The single *A.j.* 'Alba' is not so hardy as the tall pink anemones, so one has to protect it and cheer it on rather than beat it back. The superb white 'Honorine Jobert,' which will make an immense four-foot clump, may be a bit hardier. When you look at a single white Japanese anemone, you say to yourself that it's the ultimate in flower beauty, until you see the double white 'Whirlwind'. 'Whirlwind' boasts flowers that have two rows of white petals (bracts) with green undersides, fourteen or fifteen in each row, and circled by deep gold stamens with a tight green button pinning everything down in the center. They have a gay ruffly dancing look about them.

Anemone japonica 'Prince Henry' is described in some catalogs as eight inches tall, but its dark rose double daisies are actually about fifteen inches. It's a fine plant that is nonetheless almost as determined a colonizer as the tall unnamed singles I've tried in vain to curb. Of the taller japonica anemones, one of the best is 'Max Vogel', standing thirty-six inches high and bearing large semidouble clear pink flowers of good substance. It is not easy to find—mine comes from Lamb Nurseries in Washington State.

These tall hybrid anemones all bloom in late summer and in fall, carrying the perennial border triumphantly through a trying period: that is, if it is a border that eschews the deep yellows and oranges that seem to be natural for that time of year. If one has separate spring, summer, and fall borders there is no problem, but if, like most of us, one has a single large area for perennials, one has to plan carefully in order to have a satisfactory amount of appropriate color after June. I, for one, draw the line at planting *Rudbeckia* 'Goldsturm', the heleniums, heliopsis, and helianthus among the pinks and mauves of the phlox. The clumps of *A. vitifolia robustissima* will start to open a month before the *hupehensis japonica*—in late July or in August. The *japonica* hybrids come on as these finish, while the phlox is still going strong, and are perfect companions for phlox if their far-from-companionable tendencies toward aggression are firmly controlled.

6

FLOWER ARRANGEMENTS IN THE BORDER

WE ARE ALWAYS TOLD in garden books—and told truly—that the effect a plant makes depends not only on how well it is grown but also on where it is placed. We are to ask ourselves, if it is planted against a wall, do the color and texture of the wall complement the color and texture of the plant, or does the wall detract from the specimen or even, in effect, cancel it out? (Hedges as backgrounds are less apt to interfere with the visual aspect of plants growing in front of them—one has only to make sure that the hedge's roots aren't stealing all the moisture and nourishment the border plants need.) And what about the neighboring plants of the specimen under discussion? Do *their* colors, textures, and growth habits enhance the subject we are placing near them? Figuring out good plant combinations is one of the more absorbing aspects of gardening.

When planning a perennial border, naturally you learn the needs of the plants. If you can give them what they need—moisture or dry grit, shade or sun, acid or lime, temperatures that they can bear—you then consider their size, growth habit, blooming period, foliage, and the color of their blossoms, if they have blossoms that count.

Delphinium 'Bellamosum'

. . . colors, textures, and
growth habits . . . Figuring
out good plant combinations
is one of the more absorbing
aspects of gardening.

When it comes to color, the blooming period is all-important; you won't be planting a yellow chrysanthemum to go with a blue iris, since they bloom at different times of the year. You'll be looking for early veronicas, perhaps, or aquilegias that will harmonize with the iris, and for asters, plumbago, or tall sedums to put near your chrysanthemums.

Sometimes the weather will thwart you and your carefully thought out combinations by making individuals bloom sooner or later than their expected time. I had a new repetition-of-color scheme one year, planting huge, hot-pink lythrums in the back of the border where they would be repeating the color of several Veronica 'Red Fox' that were in the foreground. Unfortunately, we had a sopping season—rain came sluicing down every day or so. The lythrums, swamp plants at heart, joyfully shot up and exploded into their most flamboyant display long before the veronicas, disheartened at having to sit in mud eternally, got around to their rather sad performance. You can't win them all.

On the other hand, the plants themselves sometimes make decisions that turn out to be better than our own. We all have our ideas about which colors look good with which. I think the national approach to color combinations has broadened a lot in the last twenty years, due perhaps to Asian influence. We no longer confine ourselves to combining colors that are opposite one another on the color wheel but have been experimenting with those that are on the same side of the wheel—pink with tangerine, or purple and blue with green. Nevertheless, I certainly would never have purposely created the blend that appeared one year amid my hot colors, a deep yellow helenium, a deep yellow double helianthus, and flaming red and yellow chrysanthemums. Apparently, when I moved the helenium from the nursery, I inadvertently got a piece of an adjacent physostegia, the false dragonhead, which is of a dime-store purply pink, decidedly unrefined and the last thing to put near deep yellow, orange, and cadmium red. Yet when the physostegia, after several years, emerged jauntily in the midst of this group and I was swooping over to jerk it out, something stayed my hand. I could scarcely believe it – it looked really splendid.

If a successful combination is accidental instead of planned, we may be weak enough to register quiet pride when a visitor compliments us on our skill. We're grateful when the plants group themselves felicitously without any help from us, certainly But when, by planning ahead, we pull off a dazzling horticultural performance, what a feeling of triumph we experience!

Such a planned arrangement in my border has been giving me great satisfaction for several years. There is a rose, 'Gruss an Aachen', about three and a half feet tall, bearing sumptuous pearly pink blossoms in June. Beside it is *Salvia argentea,* when I've been forehanded enough to get it in the previous fall (it can't be expected to behave like anything other than a biennial). This salvia has enormous gray, felty leaves and carries tall candelabra branches of white dragon's-head blossoms. Close by are two smoky rose-lavender Oriental poppies, 'Lavender Embers' (regrettable name) and 'Raspberry Queen'. On the other side of the rose a swarm of white Siberian iris take flight; in front of them airy spikes are decorated with the delicate white trumpets of St. Bruno's lily *(Anthericum ramosum).* As if all this ethereal stuff weren't enough, a froth of pale *Gypsophila* 'Pink Fairy' floats this side of the clump of anthericum. Of course, it is a fleeting masterpiece; the strange lavender poppies are soon gone, the Japanese beetles arrive to chew on the roses, the white iris and lilies withdraw after a couple of weeks, and only the gypsophila carries on.

Another successful pale arrangement in the border is under the tall arching branches of the rose 'Frühlingsgold'. A group of *Veronica gentianoides* – upright twelve-inch spikes of skim-milk blue – stands near clumps of that lovely white *Anemone sylvestris* and *Anemone palmata,* which is somewhat similar but with creamy blossoms.

Several years ago I had a great sheet of pale lavender-blue *Phlox divaricata* on the edge of the woods garden, with dark purple (so-called black) tulips planted in it. It was a great joy until grass got into it and I had to fork it all up and replant. Somehow it never looked the same again, and in the end the tulips disappeared.

There was also once a glorious gray and lavender Russian sage *(Perovskia atriplicifolia)* four or five feet tall that stood in the middle of a heath and heather bed. While it was arching out its graceful spikes, the heathers 'County Wicklow' and 'Mrs. J.A. Hamilton' were making shorter, muted-pink versions of the same design this side of it. Quite stunning, but then a red Japanese maple began to loom over the perovskia and quell its enthusiasm. . . . And there was a carpet of *Prunella* 'Loveliness Pink' under clumps of the Siberian iris 'Sparkling Rose' that was most satisfactory, the colors being almost identical . . .

As for present combinations that gratify the eye, I would nominate big bouquets of the good old *Hemerocallis* 'Hyperion' blooming with *Echinops ritro,* a match found in many a garden. The gray-blue of the globe thistle comes on just in time to complement the lemon-yellow daylily. That display lasts for many weeks. Earlier, at the edge of the woods garden, the great white salvers of *Clematis lanuginosa candida* climb high in the gray buffalo berry tree. At the foot of the tree the luminous silver and pale green *Lamium* 'Beacon Silver' spreads itself without restraint, carrying its short pink spikes fairly constantly throughout the summer. But even without flowers 'Beacon Silver' earns its place in the garden.

Although I had read that one should arrange seasonal gardens, or at least keep all the early- and late-blooming plants in separate areas of the garden, I went ahead and sprinkled the early-spring to late-autumn bloomers all through the border. It was a mistake, especially in the case of spring flowers. When the rest of the border is looking like a mud flat, lo, at the far west end appear pasqueflowers, dwarf red-violet iris, and a rosy arabis. A very good combination wasted in a wilderness of wet brown earth. I should have put them down near the woods garden, which always looks good and is approaching its big moment at the time the pasqueflowers are coming out. All the little bulbs are shooting up, and the snowdrops and bloodroot are blooming. And the deep pink *Daphne mezereum* that grows there would make a good companion for the *Anemone pulsatilla*.

There is a good late-spring group where I *did* get it all together. 'Pico', a magnificent semidouble white peony with pouffy gold stamens, blooms close to and at the same time as a fine old Ghent azalea, 'Narcissiflora'. The azalea has gray-green leaves and white, cream, and dull gold (fragrant) blossoms. Beneath it are the whorled spikes of the gold-centered 'Postford White' *Primula japonica*. To make it even more beautiful, standing among the primulas is a clump of the early dense white *Astilbe* 'Deutschland'. A veritable symphony in white.

As for colors, in the border there are blue, lemon-yellow, and white groups of veronicas, yarrows, and white campanulas. There are lots of massed pinks, lavenders, blues, and purples—*Veronica* 'Royal Blue', *Salvia nemorosa* 'Blue Queen', *Delphinium* 'Bellamosum', and the purple *Campanula glomerata* with pinks supplied by coral bells, poppies, geraniums, and later, malvas. There's a gray and wine arrangement in the woods garden with *Astilbe* 'Spinell', Japanese painted fern, and *Ajuga* 'Silver Beauty'. (Wouldn't the dark red oriental herb perilla be good there—if it could stand the shade—to pick up the wine red of the fern stems?)

For some reason—maybe it's the same mysterious reason some valuable and necessary books go out of print—the single dark-red Polyantha rose 'Donald Prior' is never listed any more. Luckily, a friend gave me two bushes she'd raised from cuttings. They glorify my border all summer long. I've backed them up with one of the best hardy artemisias, 'Lambrook Silver'. I say hardy, but it must be covered thoroughly with pine boughs during the winter. Its sprays of silver filigree make the roses look even darker and more velvety red. Double feverfews contribute masses of white, as do the fringed shastas 'Aglaya', while columbines in white and pastel colors appear here and there. This side of the roses are old bushes of lavender. In late summer stokesias, both the so-called blue and the thistly white, bloom in the foreground. On the very edge of the group are 'Silver Mound' artemisias, gray-green humps of dianthus, and white and blue Carpathian campanulas. I always try to have some deep red dianthus there to echo the color of the roses. *Dianthus* 'Zing Rose' does pretty well, but as it's not reliably hardy, I have to keep replacing the plants. The taller, fancier *D.* 'War Bonnet' is perfect, but it, too, is not able to survive our winters.

Here are some suggestions for other good color combinations. *Veronica* 'Crater Lake' and 'Royal Blue' are nice with the starry *Allium moly*, if you like true blue and clear lemon-yellow together. The allium, I must warn you, goes dormant after blooming, so its yellowing foliage must be hidden by other plants. *Achillea taygetea*, which is pale sulfur yellow, looks smashing, surprisingly enough, with that wild magenta *Lychnis coronaria*. The felty gray leaves of the lychnis must help. It is a biennial that seeds itself generously. And if you're wondering how to show off the whirly blue-gray leaves and pale mauve-pink blossoms of the *Allium senescens glaucum*, try putting it next to *Ruta* 'Blue Beauty'. The rue, by the way, looks even better in early November than it does in June. The intricately cut blue leaves almost glow in cooler weather. In zone 5 it must be protected in winter and cut sharply back in the spring.

Eryngium planum or *amethystinum*, the prickly sea holly, looks stunning in back of the low, deep blue globe thistles, *Echinops* 'Veitch's Blue' and *E. bannaticus*. Plant the tall yellow *Thermopsis caroliniana* among the single delphiniums 'Bellamosum' and 'Belladonna'. You can repeat the yellow by planting sundrops *(Oenothera fruticosa)* nearby. *Geranium wallichianum* 'Buxton's Blue' is enchanting when it sends its long trailing stems through the frothy masses of gray *Nepeta* 'Dropmore' and silver-edged thyme. *Anthemis Tinctoria* is wonderful with regal lilies.

One garden writer suggested that we pick flowers and foliage every once in a while during the growing season and pace slowly around the garden, looking for plants with which they would make good bedfellows. When we find combinations we like, we should make a note, so that in the fall or spring we will remember to shift them around. A good plan.

Sometimes one is kept so busy acting as referee—trying to keep the border plants from demolishing each other—that there is small time left for working out good color combinations. Every plant that flourishes seems to want to trail over, lean on, swallow up, or invade its fellow residents of the flower border. Of course, if your garden is of a non-labor-intensive type that is becoming increasingly popular these days, one in which each plant stands alone surrounded by a thick layer of shredded bark or chips, you don't have my problem. My garden may be a modest version of what Christopher Lloyd calls a tapestry garden—one in which the gardener allows, nay, even encourages, the plants to mingle, to wander about, and to interweave. Ideally, it has a look of neatness combined with that of wild abandon, blossoms burgeoning away and tendrils flinging themselves about, clematis climbing up through the roses, cranesbills roaming amongst the solid globes of santolina and the gray masses of lavender. Fine careless rapture.

One does, however, have to remain vigilant lest the less aggressive subjects go under without a sound. It's usually the newly introduced plants that are overlaid, newcomers not being in condition to fight off old established residents of the border. One October morning I suddenly remembered having set out, in May, a new but husky dwarf goatsbeard *(Aruncus aethusifolius)* in the shade of a rosebush. Horrified, I realized I hadn't seen it for months. I rushed out, dived under the rosebush, shoved aside colonies of those beautiful ruthless brutes, Japanese anemones, and found a small piece of ragged green lace, all that remained of the dwarf aruncus. That was an *unsuccessful* combination, thought I, as I apologetically potted up the little relic. *Never* put new small plants next to large established plants, especially stoloniferous ones. I knew that . . .

7

HARDY GERANIUMS

It's a great pity that now, when we Americans are finally beginning to take an interest in creating fine gardens, we are so limited in
our choice of plants. It is not only our climate that keeps us from
growing a wider variety of perennials but also their unavailability. It
may be our own fault; we didn't ask for them, so our nurseries didn't
bother to propagate and stock them. Not *enough* of us asked for them,
at any rate. But now we are asking, some of us even clamoring, and
what happens? A few plants a year dribble over to the United States
from Europe or Japan, for some reason nearly always to the same
high-priced nursery. Surely other nurseries could import plants or
start propagating them. Perhaps we should bombard these vendors
with letters as if they were congressmen.

The hardy geraniums, or cranesbills, are a case in point. Countless
species and cultivars have been gracing European gardens for dec-
ades. We are now able to buy a handful, and every year one or two
new ones are vouchsafed us. The only way to hurry the process, aside
from nagging the nursery people, is to join the American Rock Garden Society, the Royal Horticultural Society, the Alpine Garden Society (England), or the Scottish Rock Garden Club and take advantage

Geranium 'Giuseppii'

*They really are addictive, gera-
niums — winsome, obliging,
untemperamental . . .*

of their seed exchanges. Even then, of course, one can't get hold of the special cultivars or all of the garden-worthy species. But let us, as we wait for better times, cherish the ones we have.

They really are addictive, geraniums—winsome, obliging, untemperamental and, like so many of the best garden plants, largely free of disease and persecution by insects. There are annual, biennial, and perennial geraniums, but here I will deal only with the perennials, and of those only the ones that seem to be obtainable either as plants or seed.

I should probably stop and say that we aren't talking about the pot and bedding geraniums, which are really pelargoniums—the gorgeous big red and pink things. The hardy geraniums, or cranesbills, are comparatively modest, small-flowered plants, one of which almost everyone is familiar with: *Geranium maculatum*. Our native woods geranium, it has deeply cut leaves and pale lavender blossoms. The pretty weed herb Robert is another species of the same genus. There are wild geraniums in other parts of the world, however, that put on a better show than do ours. It is these and their special forms and hybrids that are under discussion.

In geraniums there is something for everyone. There are small ones for border edges and rock gardens, those of medium height, and tall ones, although none taller than three feet. Their foliage varies in size, design, color, and texture; it is sometimes aromatic and always attractive. In many of the species it turns red in the autumn. The flowers are small but usually copious enough to make a definite contribution to the garden symphony, the colors ranging from white through pale pink, lavender, and blue to a fierce magenta, the latter, although splendid, requiring tactful handling.

Many cranesbills tolerate dry shade, making them a boon to gardeners who have such a problem site. Almost all of them will accept and even welcome part shade. They are excellent subjects to mass at the base of shrubs or to use in underplanting shrub roses. Some bloom in early spring, but most have one big blossom festival in June, a few of them performing again if cut back. Several especially generous individuals bloom all season long, earning our fervent gratitude.

The propagation of geraniums is by spring-sown seed, by cuttings taken in summer, by root cuttings of some species, and by division. Cranesbills get their name from the seed-carrying part of the plant, which is shaped like the bill of a crane (and *geranos* means "crane" in Greek). It consists of a little five-sectioned chamber, the rostrum, from which emerges a long, thin central column whose exterior is covered by five separate strips, or awns, that act as springs. It's a tricky device; when the seed is ripe the rostrum starts to separate into the seed-holding sections, called mericarps. The awns suddenly peel away from the bottom and curl upward, each awn taking its mericarp with it and shooting the seed into the air. If you intend to harvest your own seed, you must look sharp lest the plant disperse it before you get there, leaving only the empty crane's bills. There's a crucial period just when the seed is dry but before the explosion takes place.

Some hybrids, of course, are sterile, and others produce seed that will not as a rule come true: that is, they will not reproduce the parent. With the species you are sure of getting the same plant with only slight variations.

Division is easy with most geraniums and is best done either in spring or right after they finish flowering in July. The ones that never finish flowering must be divided in spring, obviously. Harper and McGourty say that if you want new plants of border geraniums, you can burrow down under them with your fingers and break off pieces from the mother plant.* If they say so, it must be so, but I've never tried it. My soil is probably too solid for such a neat operation. The method might work well in sandy loam, especially with *G. sanguineum* and all its cultivars, which manufacture so many fleshy roots.

---

*Harper, Pamela, and Frederick McGourty, *Perennials: How to Select, Grow, and Enjoy.* Tucson: HP Books (1985).

Two of the most popular geraniums in circulation today are culti-vars of *G. cinereum* – *G.c.* 'Ballerina' and *G.c. subcaulescens* 'Splendens'. The first is Alan Bloom's doll of a plant, a four-inch mound of gray-green five-parted lobed leaves that carries, from June on, one-and-a-half-inch open-cup flowers of smoky pink. The petals are notched on the edges and are veined with purply wine red. There is also a wine-red patch at the base. Sadly, one isn't told by its vendors that this is definitely a rock garden plant and should be planted up high in a suitably gritty soil or at the very least in sandy, well-drained loam on level ground. I lost several of them from the front of the border during long rainy periods.

I'd like to find the species *G. cinereum*, which comes from the Pyrenees. It is a rosette plant with grayish leaves, white- or pink-veined flowers, and long trailing stems, so it can cascade over a wall. The species *G.c. subcaulescens*, from Turkey, is also good for sheeting over walls and is "a really splendid plant for those not afraid to admire a dazzling colour," says Peter Yeo, the final authority on geraniums. The flowers are magenta with a black area in the center. The plant that is offered by nurseries is a cultivar of this: *G.c.s.* 'Splendens', a charming little nontrailing rosette whose ferocious blossoms must be of the hottest pink in the world. Brilliant but not harsh, slightly iridescent with a blackish-red basal blotch, it also should be grown under rock garden conditions, perhaps surrounded by gray-foliaged plants and small blue campanulas. It should *not* be set down in soggy clay.

Another small plant for a raised bed or wall garden is a six-inch Yugoslav, *Geranium dalmaticum*, which makes tiny tufted clumps of small glossy, lobed, fan-shaped leaves. The flowers are of a most re-fined pale pink, untainted by even a whiff of magenta. We are told that where summers are of reasonable temperatures, it should be grown in grit in full sun; where summers are searingly hot, it wants moist soil in part shade.

You can easily find the one-and-a-half-foot species *Geranium en-dressii*, its several special forms, and the hybrids to which it has contributed. The cultivar most readily available is 'Wargrave Pink', although my favorite is 'A.T. Johnson'. They both grow fifteen to eighteen inches high, have deeply lobed five-part leaves like those of a buttercup, and flower all summer. 'Wargrave Pink' has candy-pink blooms, and 'A.T. Johnson' has flowers of silvery salmon-pink containing no blue. The cultivars have one habit that you might find annoying: after their initial burst of bloom in spring, they send masses of new blossoming stems out from under the central tuft of foliage, which means they take up about one foot more space all the way around than you had allotted them. Their neighbors either fight back or sink soundlessly out of sight. You will say to yourself in August, "Whatever happened to those blue salvias?" When you lift up the skirts of 'Wargrave' or 'A.T. Johnson', you'll find out. Some people plant these cranesbills near tolerant shrubs into which they may climb. But probably if one were to cut these plants to the ground after the first flowering, they wouldn't have to resort to any rude tactics to keep blooming and would simply send up new, nicely restrained flowering clumps. One might be brave and try it. The species is not so rampant but has mauve-pink blossoms.

Geranium endressii was crossed with *G. versicolor* to make *G. oxonianum* 'Claridge Druce', a vigorous plant that grows quite tall for a cranesbill—two and a half to three feet. The foliage is somewhat hairy and slightly glossy, and the flowers are funnel shaped and rosy pink with a strong network of dark veins, the color fading to white at the base. This plant has two outstanding virtues—it likes shade and it comes true from seed.

A really superior plant that has *endressii* for one parent is *G. riversleaianum* 'Russell Prichard'. It is said to be marginally hardy, since the lovely but tender *G. traversii* is its other parent, but I've kept it cheerful in my border for three or four years. I've read that it likes a dry sunny spot, so I plan to put a piece of it on a rock wall. Its ebullience is unquenchable—cataracts of bright pink flowers flow from it all summer and fall. Because their color has magenta in it and is brighter than that of either parent, it has been wrongly assumed to have *G. sanguineum* forebears. I cover it tenderly in winter and lift off the pine boughs with much trepidation every spring. It should be divided and replanted every few years. I long to have *G. riversleanianum* 'Mavis Simpson', which is described as a sort of sister to 'Russell Prichard' with shell-pink blooms.

Another case of mistaken genealogy is the assignment of fifteen- to eighteen-inch *Geranium* 'Johnson's Blue' to the *endressii* group, when it is actually, according to expert analysis, a cross between *himalayense* and *pratense*. This well-known sterile hybrid, like so many of the taller geraniums, forms a wonderful hemisphere of deeply divided leaves until it blooms, when the perfect filigreed half-globe is destroyed. You do have the comfort of the good violet-blue flowers, which are almost one and a half inches across, with translucent veins and pinkish tones, especially towards the base. One nursery says the flowers bloom from May to September, but actually they cover June and part of July. If you plant a swath of 'Johnson's Blue' in front of a mass of the 'Helen Elizabeth' Oriental poppy, I can promise you an exhilarating aesthetic experience.

Backing up to *Geranium himalayense*, we hit a confusion of nomenclature that I am tempted to spare you. On second thought, you'd better learn if you don't already know that it is sold also under the names *grandiflorum* and *meeboldii*. Without this knowledge one may buy the same thing two or three times, paying dearly for one's ignorance. I did just that last summer, which is one of the reasons I decided to straighten myself out on the geranium situation. *G. himalayense* is also fifteen to eighteen inches tall and produces the largest and the most intensely blue flowers of any cranesbill. They are still violet blue, it is true, but Graham Thomas says they are "like butterflies, beautifully veined." I have only one I got as *grandiflorum alpinum*, which I am told is not quite so gorgeous as *himalayense* proper. They bloom from June to August. After they have finished blooming, these plants can be cut to the ground, after which they will quickly make fresh new foliage but will not bloom again. There is a double one marketed either as *G. grandiflorum* 'Plenum' (*G. himalayense* 'Plenum') or 'Birch Double' that sports mauve pouffes.

While we are dealing with the blues, consider *Geranium* 'Magnificum', which Dr. Yeo calls the king of the cranesbills. It has always been my favorite blue one during the years I didn't know its name, so I was glad to see it lauded. Often labeled *G. platyphyllum* or *G. ibiricum* or *platypetalum,* though it is a sterile hybrid of the last two plants, it is two feet tall and has sticky, hairy flower stalks and handsome, deeply cut hairy rounded leaves of good substance, which usually turn red in fall. The large blue, red-veined flowers are, I think, even prettier than those of 'Johnson's Blue'. All of these taller geraniums need frequent division, as they spread fast.

Geranium pratense, the handsome European and Asian meadow cranesbill that is the tallest of them all, comes in blue, too, but it's a gray or lavender blue. The plant is really too much of an oaf for the border, at least for mine, for it flops open as it flowers—if only it would retain its elegant dome shape! It also seeds itself with what has been called "feckless fecundity." All in all, the unadulterated species is surely a candidate for the wild garden, where it can naturalize itself and be welcome to the space it takes up. I do have *G. pratense* 'Plenum Violaceum', a bulky plant that doesn't seed itself and has charming double red-violet blossoms. There exists 'Plenum Album', too, and *B.p.* 'Mrs. Kendall Clark', which some say is blue and some say pearl gray or flushed rose.

I have, thanks to British seed exchanges, raised a few plants of *Geranium wallichianum* and *G.w.* 'Buxton's Variety', sometimes called 'Buxton's Blue', which I also hover over, fearing they will leave me bereft some cold winter night. They are from the Himalayas but are undoubtedly not accustomed to capricious and violent weather changes, especially without the protection of snow. Low mound plants with interesting marbled leaves, their endless trailing stems produce an endless supply of one-inch flowers with scalloped petals that in cool weather are quite delicious. (Heat turns them mauve.) The outer edges are iridescent blue shading to crimson toward the center, where there is a circle of pale cool white, the whole thing traced with faint wine-red veins. A cluster of dark, wine-colored stamens whose anthers are navy blue completes this little masterpiece. The underside is of rosy lavender veined with dark red. One should place 'Buxton's Variety' on a wall or in a well-drained spot in the front of the border near a friendly neighbor whose foliage will be complementary and who won't object to being laced with the wandering stems of the cranesbill. Grey santolinas are compatible, or small white shrub potentillas. *Nepeta* 'Dropmore', perhaps. Lavender? *G. wallichianum* has a deep tap root so is difficult to move once established. Since it doesn't easily divide, the usual method of propagation is by seeds.

In my garden are a few more seed-exchange geraniums that haven't yet bloomed – *G. psilostemon (armenum)*, a tall vibrant magenta-flowering subject, and *G. pylzowianum,* an alpine from China that will not survive if Wyman's zone 7 warning is accurate. Lincoln Foster describes it so enticingly that I'm hoping Wyman exaggerates. Foster says it creeps about bearing lovely flat, clear-pink blossoms on thin wiry stems one to two inches above its foliage. It wants a starvation diet and full sun. Of *G. renardii* I have only one specimen and it doesn't look quite satisfied. Its foliage and mounded compact structure make it worth growing; the grayish leaves are circular, puckered, and deeply lobed. The flowers are described as brief – on my plant they were also sparse, consisting of pale, divided cups with lilac veins. Ingwersen calls them "starry opal white." Well, maybe in his garden. This one wants a rock garden and hates fat soil, which may have been my problem.

I've been trying to keep *G. macrorrhizum* 'Ingwersen's Variety' from surging all over its part of the border, but now that I've learned it is used as an effective ground cover in dry shade I see my solution. Although the pale pink flowers on this ten-inch plant are not dazzling, the divided, rounded, light green leaves are fruitily aromatic as well as pretty. (They were formerly used for oil of geranium.) I'd like to get 'Album,' whose white flowers have red calyces, and 'Bevan's Variety', which is crimson purple.

At last it is possible in this country to obtain *Geranium phaeum*, the so-called mourning widow. Other nurseries may have it, but I found it for the first time listed by the fine new California nursery, Canyon Creek. The murky blackish-purple blossoms of this plant are small—intriguing rather than flashy—but those of the cultivar 'Lily Lovell' are really quite pretty. The plant itself appears handsomer and more vigorous than the species.

What *is* offered here in quantity is *Geranium sanguineum* and all its forms and special cultivars. It's called "bloody cranesbill" in England, from its botanical name. I can't think why, as its bright magenta flowers are far from reminding one of blood. The species, usually one and a half to two feet high, makes a kind of dense, twiggy, fast-spreading shrub of starry leaves covered with five-petaled flowers of a shade that is not currently fashionable. Flaming reds, purples, and magentas will no doubt become more popular as we refined gardeners work through our pastel period and gradually allow ourselves to enjoy brilliant color. There are a couple of very good dwarf forms of this cranesbill sold by a rock garden nursery, and 'Shepherd's Warning' ("sunrise pink") recently arrived from England at another nursery. The double ones are not here yet, but 'Album' *is* here, and I love it,

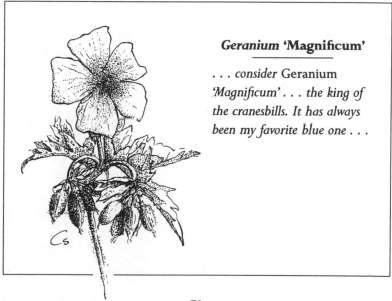

Geranium 'Magnificum'

. . . consider Geranium *'Magnificum' . . . the king of the cranesbills. It has always been my favorite blue one . . .*

despite its colonizing impulses, for its really pure white airy, delicate blossoms. The one most people prefer is *G.s.* 'Striatum' *(lancastriense)*, which is found either in mound or prostrate form. It has pointed divided leaves and pale apple-blossom-pink flowers veined red. Couldn't be more refined. A mass of flowers is produced in spring; then a few appear off and on all summer.

I have not dealt with all the garden cranesbills available in this country, having left out *G. sylvaticum* 'Mayflower', as well as the tiny brown-foliaged *G. sessiliflorum* 'Nigricans' and the pink-flowered rock plant *G. orientalitibeticum,* which has marbled leaves and round tubers strung together on ever-advancing roots, making them look like strings of prayer beads. And probably a few others – but there are so many more not yet available. What are the nurserymen waiting for?

8

THE STRUGGLE FOR CONTROL

*I will go root away the noisome weeds, that without profit suck
the soil's fertility from wholesome flowers.*

—Richard III

SOME GARDEN AUTHORITIES SAY that four essentials of good gardens
are perfect lawns, paths, hedges, and walls. That sounds like a big
order, but they also say, quite accurately, that flowers need a good
setting, that the garden must not look unkempt, that one cannot
obtain a feeling of serenity if the aspect is that of a place not under
control. I quote Miss Jekyll in *Wall and Water Gardens:* "The purpose
of a garden is to give happiness and repose of mind."

It is true that I obtained happiness and even repose of mind in an
old, neglected Turkish garden that surrounded our house in North
Africa, but that was because it had achieved the melancholic charm
of ancient ruins. The terraces and high walls were soft with moss;
geraniums (pelargoniums) had gone wild on the overgrown slopes;
archways were festooned with wild clematis; little pink and lavender

Garden in Algiers

*. . . I obtained happiness and
even repose of mind in an old,
neglected Turkish garden
that surrounded our house in
North Africa . . . it had
achieved the melancholic
charm of ancient ruins.*

stonecrops decorated the stairways; yellow jasmine and milky blue plumbago cascaded over banks, all intertwined, while a wisteria climbed to the very top of a cypress. Sometimes a large, gold-patterned snake would hang in the sunshine from the loops of giant aloes that draped one terrace wall. Arums, the yellow Italian one and the huge, sinister-looking *A. dracunculus,* hid their hooded clubs in the shadowy tangles. Pistacia bushes filled the air with a heady, resinous odor. The plants had it all their own way—those, that is, that didn't appeal to the small flocks of sheep and goats that often crept in and browsed among them, or to our donkey, a permanent resident. The joy one felt in that garden was tinged with sadness because one was surrounded by the ruins of former splendor—the same sadness in a lesser degree that one feels standing among the toppled stones of old Ionian cities. Yet one is happy because it's so lovely, even in its state of decay. And one feels repose because the struggle between man and Nature has been resolved: Nature has won.

Now dilapidation is all very well in a spot that contains venerable relics of a former civilization, especially around the Mediterranean, where things seem to fall apart gracefully. The English at one period tried deliberately to provoke the subtle blend of emotions by duplicating ancient ruins in their gardens. I have the feeling it didn't quite come off. Nor will a weedy, untended, unorganized modern garden produce anything other than distress in owner and visitor alike. This reality poses a problem for people with property but without gardeners.

If a homeowner would like a garden but doesn't like physical labor, and he is of but moderate means, he had better put everything in grass (gravel, if he lives in the Southwest) and buy a riding mower. Or he can plant his property with trees, shrubs, and perhaps a few of the garden designers' favorite workhorse perennials: hemerocallis (daylilies), hostas, *Rudbeckia* 'Goldsturm', *Sedum* 'Autumn Joy', and decorative but noninvasive grasses, all of which perform their assignments infallibly and endure neglect courageously.

Someone who has not much free time but enjoys working outdoors and would like to experiment with perennials could limit himself to a twenty-foot border or island bed. It really would not require much more time to maintain than the same area of lawn, as flowers are willing to wait a while for attention but the grass must be mowed when it reaches a certain height—which it seems to do twice a week in May and June—to say nothing of weeding and feeding, if you go in for that sort of thing.

Then the thing to do is to choose plants that give pleasure but that don't require hovering over—plants that are not invasive, that don't need spraying or staking.

Ah, but if you find gardening a joy and you have the time and space, you can create a huge mixed border of shrubs and perennials and spend many hours learning the blooming periods of each plant and orchestrating the colors. The work is play when you love it. If you study garden books, you will find lots of information and suggestions, most of them good.

Various panaceas are offered by the experts for solving the weed problems every gardener will encounter. (Even people who like to weed may have more of it than they can keep up with.) One of them is the use of ground covers.

Now pachysandra and English ivy are doing well here in shady spots, where few weeds are eager to follow them. But as the ultimate solution to the weed problem, ground covers have been vastly over-rated, especially for a sunny spot. You have to go on weeding most of them for several years, until they become established, and it's more difficult to weed a ground cover than to mow grass or hoe bare soil. It helps if you have access to thick, weed-free mulch with which to surround each new plant. Some of the ground covers do eventually grow thick and strong enough to keep out the weeds—in other people's gardens. Vinca is one of the best. It grows in sun or shade, it spreads quite fast, it has very pretty flowers in spring, and it looks shiny and tidy most of the year. In a city or suburban landscape, where the Enemy consists of only a few tribes of weeds, it may prevail. Here on my farm, however, it surrenders to grasses, poison ivy, Virginia creeper, burdock, black raspberry brambles, and several other invaders with which I am very familiar but whose names I don't know.

There is a pretty, creeping, blue-flowered ground cover, *Veronica pectinata,* of which I am very fond, but grass from the lawn sneaks up under it and waves in long spears above the soft green mat if I am not vigilant, and then I have another transplanting job. The same is true of the lovable creeping thymes and even the tight-woven *Mazus reptans* with lavender blossoms like tiny snapdragons. It creeps into the grass and the grass into it. If I plant the creepers away from the edge of the lawn, weed seeds blow into them and take hold that way.

The books say that these ground covers compete successfully with grass, but that simply is not true—not with *my* grass. Of course, mine is a particularly difficult situation; it's a garden made in an ex-pasture. When I prepared the soil, I removed every last weed and root, but presumably, even after many years, the weed seeds are still viable. Then, too, the garden is even now surrounded by high weeds. I keep pushing back the jungle, little by little, but it hasn't been pushed very far as yet. One of the worst airborne invaders is the seed of dame's rocket *(Hesperis matronalis),* which abounds on this property. Its white and lavender phloxlike flowers are pretty and fragrant, but its seedlings come up by the thousands in the garden. It's an all-too-naturalized European, like the English sparrow.

Sometimes ground covers turn out to be more of a problem than the weeds they were meant to control. In my search for ground covers I once sent away and actually paid for a curse called *Polygonum cuspidatum compactum (reynoutria),* or fleece flower. Reputable nurseries sell this bully of a plant, supplying dazzling pictures of what are actually negligible reddish sepals, not even proper flowers. In the garden it began to travel at such an alarming rate that it was soon apparent I would have to initiate a counterattack. It was impossible to dig out, since its huge roots go down under the roots of shrubs and trees. I fought the thing in vain until I learned of the herbicide that kills by traveling down from the leaves to the roots without poisoning the soil. I spread plastic over all the nearby plants, then dipped the leaves of the polyganum into a jar of the herbicide solution. Three repetitions of this treatment resulted in victory at last.

One method of cutting the weeding time is by using mulch. It does help control weeds and conserves moisture at the same time. The fact that it encourages slugs and mice is a drawback, but you can't have everything, can you? So mulch where you can – some plants like it and others don't. Heavy feeders, such as phlox and delphinium, love a top dressing or mulch of old manure. But plants that ordinarily grow on rocky cliffs, such as cheddar pinks, drabas, some silenes, the gray, furry rock yarrows, and other saxatile plants want a mulch only of stone chips, if anything. Certainly not a collar that will turn mushy.

There is a growing practice of mulching everything – trees, shrubs, and perennials – with shredded bark, wood chips, or sawdust. I think the bark and chips are excellent around trees or shrubs, but I would not want to use them in the perennial border for several reasons. One, if they are fresh, they take nitrogen from the soil while they are decomposing. Two, even if they are well rotted, they may be highly acid and would not be greeted with joy by delphiniums, pinks, and other lovers of limy or neutral soil. They could be tested for acidity and lime could be added, I suppose. Some gardeners use unrotted chips and even fresh sawdust as a mulch on their flower gardens by adding blood meal to them, but I am leery of the practice myself – I've had such disastrous results, especially with sawdust mulches.

My hunch that bark mulches are no good for the perennial border was fortified when I attended a cooperative extension seminar for perennial growers in 1987. There we learned that bark and wood chip mulches have been found to rot the stems of some perennials. We were therefore advised to keep it well away from the stems – but not, of course, to stop using it entirely, since it saves work.

My final reason is that wood chips and bark in the perennial border could well deprive me of the self-seeded progeny of flax, delphinium, and many other desirable plants. How could the seeds push down and the young plants push up through the thick, inhos-

pitable layer? And what about the offspring of such annuals as cyno-
glossum and poppies, the migrants of the garden? They would find it
impossible to carry on, and what a loss that would be!

I am at present happily mulching with rotted silage, a gift from a
neighboring farmer. It is, apparently, the perfect solution: Having
been fermented, it contains no weed seeds, and it is dark, fine tex-
tured, fluffy, and nourishing. All farmers clean the old silage out of
their silos before putting in a fresh batch; perhaps other gardeners
could obtain it inexpensively.

If you don't mulch, plan to go over the whole planted area thoroughly with a hoe or other cultivating tool about three times during
the growing season. Do it once in early spring after all the perennials
have surfaced. (If you mark the slow emergers, such as balloon flowers and Japanese anemones, the fall before, you won't destroy them
during your cleanup operations.) Then cultivate again in late spring to
get the new crop of weeds while they're still small. In July you may
have to pull some weeds, especially in the front of the border where
they show, but there will be less ground exposed by then, so less work
to do. The first two weedings in the spring are the most important.
The thing is to get the weeds while they're tiny. Once your flowers
shoot up and spread out, there will hardly be a spot for a weed to
grow in, and you can easily pull those that do appear. Also try to
scratch among the plants after every rain wherever the earth is exposed, to conserve moisture and avoid cracks in the soil. Doing so
seems to encourage the plants mightily and discourage the weeds.
Finally, a good cleanup in the fall will cut down your work the
following spring.

9

SALVIAS

To MOST PEOPLE salvia means the ubiquitous annual from Brazil, *Salvia splendens,* whose shaggy spikes of flaming relentless red, whether lining front walks or marching in circles and squares in parks and suburban gardens, afflict our eyes much of the summer in all parts of the United States. These plants have been the delight not only of suburbanites but also of plant breeders who have produced them tall and short, fat and thin, and now even in various colors—white, pink, rose, lilac, and purple. The most popular ones, however, still come from the garden centers and supermarkets in flats labeled 'Red Blazer' or 'Early Bonfire.'

But *salvia,* which means "sage," comprises a whole world of plants that wouldn't remind the average observer even faintly of the red tide that has been loosed on us from *Salvia splendens.* There are such charming plants among them that in discussing them, the real salvia fan scarcely knows where to begin. Or where to stop. It would be helpful for northern gardeners, perhaps, to deal only with the hardy varieties, but there are lots of fascinating exotic, nonhardy varieties that one would not like to leave out. They can be grown as annuals or biennials and preserved by means of seed or cuttings or by bringing them indoors for the winter.

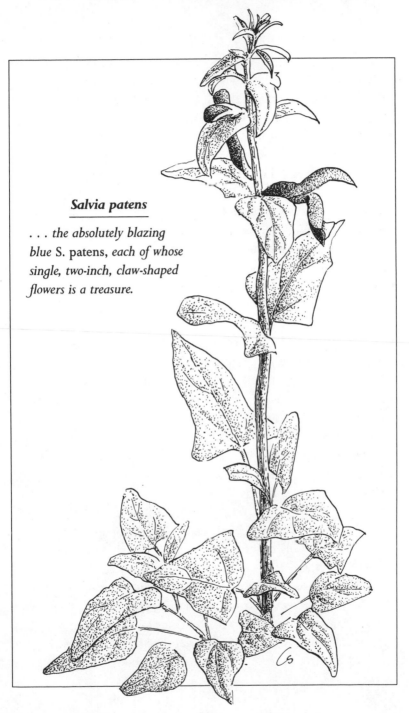

Salvia patens

. . . *the absolutely blazing*
blue S. patens, *each of whose*
single, two-inch, claw-shaped
flowers is a treasure.

Let us be organized by stating at the outset that salvias are of the *Labiatae,* or mint, family. Many but not all species of *Labiatae* are aromatic (savory, marjoram, thyme, balm, and the mints are cultivated herbs from this family). The 750 species of the genus *Salvia* include annuals, biennials, perennials, shrubs, and subshrubs, the leaves of some of which are used for flavoring. They come from all over the temperate and tropical regions of the earth, many being native to the Americas. Like other members of their family, they have dragon's-head blossoms, lipped and hooded; their leaves are opposite; their flowers are in whorls; and their stems are usually square.

All salvias want full sun, or as close to it as possible, and all but one of those I will mention here insist on good drainage. Since many of them have hairy stems and leaves that conserve moisture, they do not suffer badly during droughts, and since most of them come from stony, comparatively barren sites, they do not require rich food.

As for hardy salvias, there are actually very few that can be depended on to live through a northern winter. Foremost among them is a plant of great garden value whose origin is in such a state of confusion that I have no intention of trying to sort it out. It is a hybrid that is usually sold as *Salvia superba* or *S. nemorosa superba* (although it may be *S. virgata nemorosa*), a very fine individual that grows from two to three feet tall and carries its red-violet spikes for many weeks, starting in June. These spikes, emerging from a low woody tuft of pungent crenelated leathery leaves, are close set with wine-red bracts and purple-violet corollas. One problem is that as the flower spikes finish their performance, they remain a nice wine-dregs color that still contributes positively to the garden, making it difficult to force oneself to remove them. If, however, one courageously cuts off each spike separately at its base, fresh flowers will continue to spring up way into fall. There are several cultivars of this plant for sale, all of them shorter than the original except for 'Blue Queen' which, as raised from seed, seems to me to be identical to *S. superba* itself. 'East Friesland' ('Ostfriesland') is around sixteen inches, nicely compact;

'May Night' ('Mainacht') is said by one grower to be twelve to fourteen inches, by another, eighteen. I have not yet obtained it but would like to, as it is described enthusiastically by one and all. *Salvia superba* or *S.s.* 'Blue Queen' you can easily grow from seed. The other two are available from nurseries, or you might persuade a friend to divide his specimens some spring; they'll be all the better for it because, like so many plants, *S. superba* holds its flower stems up straighter if it is divided fairly regularly.

One spring I planted seeds of the new *S.s.* 'Rose Queen', proudly lined the stout young plants out in the nursery, only to be terribly disappointed the following year when they bloomed. Such wishy-washy, pinkish, characterless plants! My helper and I kept hoping they'd become more attractive as the season wore on, but no such thing. We ended by pulling them all out and throwing them on the compost, wailing about all the time we'd wasted on them.

Aside from the culinary sage, *Salvia officinalis,* there seems to be only one other truly hardy salvia readily available, *S. azurea* var. *grandiflora,* sold as *S. pitcheri,* an American native from South Carolina to Texas. In *Taylor's Guide to Perennials* it's said to be suitable for zone 6, even then needing protection in winter, whereas Wyman lists it for zone 4. Here on the colder edge of zone 5 it overwinters easily, so I'm inclined to think Taylor too prudent in this case. *S. pitcheri* is a salvia I wouldn't be without, although I am far from being able to keep it erect—or even to help it flop gracefully. The books say to cut it back by half when it's about fifteen inches high, but since it already blooms so late that it's blasted by frost in the midst of its splendor, should one really delay it further by cutting it back? Or will cutting it back not make it bloom later? So far I haven't dared try. I've tried staking it one way and another and last year grew it through metal hoops, but I can't say it looked at its ease either way. Its long, slender stems just refuse to cooperate, and its small, slim, pointed leaves don't even begin to conceal one's pathetic prosthetic devices. Next year (how often we gardeners say "next year") I'm going to use the hoops again but plant bushy things around the base of the plants. If you have ever seen the celestial blue blossoms of this salvia, you won't be wondering why someone would make such an effort to control the gangly thing.

There is another sage that's reputedly hardy, *Salvia jurisicii,* from Yugoslavia. Eighteen inches or one foot tall, depending on what book you're looking in, and wide spreading, its stems carry spikes of upside-down violet-blue flowers. I don't know why they are upside down. But I do know that they're not the only plant with this habit, as there's even a word for it—resupinate. Sounds very odd, *S. jurisicii,* besides being hard to find. Still, I'd like to find it.

Salvia haematodes, which is sometimes listed as a variant of the European meadow clary, *S. pratensis,* is such a fine plant that it's a pity it must be treated as a biennial, at least in cold climates. It's one of those salvias that send tall (two- to three-feet), almost leafless candelabra flower stems up from a basal rosette of large, coarse, wrinkled, hairy leaves. The flowers are of a cloudy pale lavender, highly aromatic and loved by bees. I like to put these in front of a mass of *Delphinium* 'Bellamosum'. Of course, when the show's over and the salvias and delphiniums must be cut back, you have a Problem Area, at least until the delphiniums send up new spikes. Special cultivars of *S. haematodes* are in circulation—'Indigo' and 'Midsummer', dark and pale indigo, respectively. I wonder if they come true from seed? I'd hate to buy a plant only to have it disappear during the winter, leaving no young that resembled it.

The frankly biennial *Salvia sclarea,* or clary sage, is very similar to *S. haematodes*—in fact, the only apparent difference among the seedlings is that the clary leaf is somewhat shorter and rounder. It attains the same height as *haematodes* and has the same growth habits, but its flowers are less attractive, being whitish and lilac, except for *S.s. turkestaniana,* which is a very handsome variety with white and pink flowers. Clary sage is a most useful herb, having long been the source of an aromatic oil that is used in medicine and for flavoring wines and perfume.

If you let *haematodes* and *sclarea* seed themselves, you'll have flowers every other year, as you probably already know, but if you gather some of the seeds yourself and plant them every year, you'll have flowers every year. Somehow I rarely get around to doing this.

The basal rosette of *Salvia argentea* is almost startling in its size and texture. The thick, irregularly lobed, furry silver leaves are about a foot long—enormous creatures. They look almost alive. You should plant this salvia near the front of the border or group of plants so that the leaves can be seen and appreciated. Many American gardeners cut off the tall branching stems with their white flowers (grey-white calyx and white hood), but most British gardeners consider the plant statuesque and let the flowers remain. *S. argentea* is one of those exasperating plants that we are told is a perennial but that should be treated like a biennial.

Even though it comes from Spain, the Balkans, and Asia Minor, *Salvia officinalis*, our cooking sage, is hardy. It will grow over two feet high and only needs trimming back in spring to remain tidy. The dwarf form, *S.o.* 'Compacta,' is also hardy and makes a fine gray border plant. There are other beautiful cultivars—whether hybrids or not I cannot discover—but the sad fact is that none of them are hardy. *S.o.* 'Purpurascens' is deep purple overlaid with gray; 'Icterina' is yellow and gray; but the best, to my mind, is 'Tricolor,' a heady combination of red, pink, cream, gray, and purple. I find it so gorgeous that I'm willing to pot it up and overwinter it in the cold frame or the glassed-in back porch.

Lots of herb gardeners grow pineapple sage *(S. elegans* or *S. rutilans)*, although it can't be wintered over out-of-doors north of zones 9 and 10. The light green ovate, pointed, deliciously fragrant leaves are very good in fruit drinks and salads during the summer, and it makes an attractive three-foot to four-foot branching plant. The maddening thing is that its slender, velvety, scarlet flowers don't emerge until just before the first frost, when the whole structure collapses like lettuce under boiling water. One fall years ago, when I still had time for such nonsense, I plopped a whole enormous plant into a pot and trundled it into the parlor so I could for once enjoy the blossoms. I did enjoy them, sitting before it as before a Christmas tree. But since it took up a large part of the parlor that winter, I didn't repeat the performance. Cuttings of pineapple sage root readily, even in water, especially if you take them in spring or summer.

Salvia clevelandii, from California, is admired by many and is even used as a substitute for *S. officinalis* in cooking. It is admittedly a stunning gray plant, but I find its odor most offensive; I had to evict the plant I had in the dead of winter, which made me feel like a wicked stepmother. Two salvias from Mexico I adore—*S. involucrata* and *S. leucantha.* From small rooted cuttings they form, in one summer, enormous shrubs—subshrubs, actually. *Leucantha* has pointed linear leaves that are woolly white on the underside and bears woolly racemes of white flowers encased in violet-purple calyces. It's pungent, too, but pleasantly so. *Involucrata* has rich green toothed, velvety leaves on dark red stems and produces the most amazing inflorescences with pink, knobby bracts surrounding buds that burst into large, cerise-crimson flowers. I grew one of these plants last summer up through a 'New Dawn' rose, which is of a most restrained pale pearly pink. The explosions of uninhibited Mexican color in its midst were just what that rose needed. The branches of *S. involucrata* go to such extravagant lengths that they are inclined to break off next to the main stem, so the support of the rose was helpful. Cuttings can be taken of both these salvias before the weather turns cold and rooted indoors for garden use next spring. I don't know whether *leucantha* will root in water, but *involucrata* will. I have lots of them right now that have been transferred into pots and are growing so fast they're shouldering their fellow plants out of the sun space in the bay windows. I keep cutting them back—it will be a relief when I can plant them outside in spring, like releasing wild birds from a cage.

There is a South American native, *Salvia uliginosa,* which I suppose would flourish year-round in our southern states but here must be grown as an annual. It attains five feet or more and needs support in the form of a fence or shrubs over which it can fling its long sprays of true blue flowers. This is one salvia that likes damp soil. I haven't grown it but have seen it luxuriating in the perennial garden at Stonecrop Nurseries in the hills above New York City. I do grow, most years, the absolutely blazing blue *S. patens,* each of whose single, two-inch claw-shaped flowers is a treasure. It has been described as a "compact plant," but in my garden it grows two and a half feet long and makes use of its neighbors for support. In addition to not getting good marks in the growth habit department, it must be lifted before a frost if you want to hang on to it, and its tuberous roots plunged into a box or bucket of sand and peat. This way it can wait for spring in a cool basement if kept slightly moist. Do not plant it out until you're very sure the frosts have finished. I bring my buckets up to the back porch about the middle of April so that any premature shoots can have light.

The annual mealy-cup sage, *Salvia farinacea,* is seen in gardens now more often than formerly. The old 'Blue Bedder', which is really lavender, not blue, grows to a bushy thirty inches and holds its many spikes erect. The newer 'Victoria' is a more intense purple or violet blue and remains at around eighteen inches. They are both good border plants, harmonizing well with most perennials, and have the extra virtue of drying to Wedgwood blue. In winter bouquets sprays of this salvia are usually taken for lavender.

Another annual, *S. viridis,* until recently *S. horminum,* is a good one to try. It produces racemes of colored bracts that are most interesting, coming in plummy grayish off-colors, at least until fairly recently. The catalogs now show pictures of these "flowers" in shades of brilliant pink and purple as well as white. They are said to dry well, too, but I can't testify to that.

People write about *Salvia glutinosa,* or Jupiter's beard, describing this three-foot hardy perennial from Europe and Asia as robust and bushy with a dense, spready growth and short spikes of pale yellow lipped flowers. It is recommended by some gardeners for rough places and is said to have handsome foliage. I wonder why one doesn't see it around? J. L. Hudson's World Seed Service has had, and may still have, seed for this plant as well as for other interesting salvias. I notice

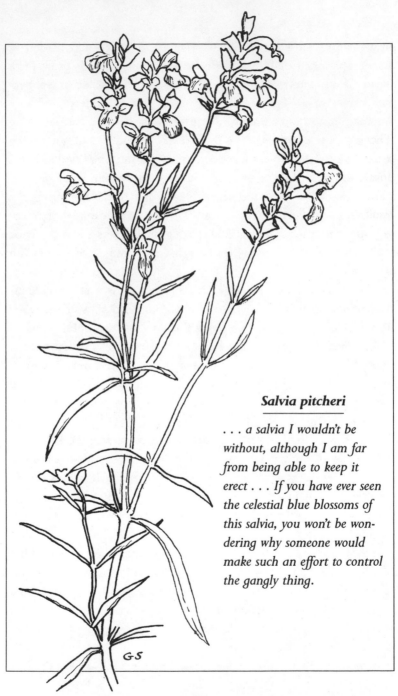

Salvia pitcheri

. . . a salvia I wouldn't be without, although I am far from being able to keep it erect . . . If you have ever seen the celestial blue blossoms of this salvia, you won't be wondering why someone would make such an effort to control the gangly thing.

in his 1986 catalog seed of *S. coccinea,* which is the next one I want to try. Since it's bright red, you'll wonder why, after my fulminating against *S. splendens.* Ah, but this one is much more subtle, spacing its small velvety scarlet blooms out on slender black three-foot stems. It has also "aromatic, downy, heart-shaped leaves," so the catalog reports. There are cultivars of this – 'Bi-Color' in white and pink and 'Lactea' in white (naturally), but I want the red one. As it's from all the hot places south, including Mexico and the West Indies, I'll have to grow it as an annual . . . unless it decides to save me the labor and start seeding itself around.

10

AVERTING CHAOS

WEEDS ARE NOT THE GARDENER'S only problem. A few other tasks must be attended to in maintaining a perennial garden, namely cutting back, edging, controlling insects and diseases, fertilizing, dividing, and, if you are growing tall plants that won't stand alone, staking.

Cutting back or removing the spent flower stems is done in the interests of tidiness and of saving the plant from expending its life forces in making seed—assuming you don't want the seed. Once a season for each kind of perennial will suffice. There are some perennials, however, that will bloom twice a season if they are cut back immediately after flowering: delphiniums, some dianthus, some gypsophilas, lavender. Other plants will bloom nearly all summer if you have the time to deadhead them, that is, cut off the dead flower heads: among them, coral bells (heuchera), balloon flowers (platycodon), red valerian *(Centranthus ruber)*, the Carpathian bellflower *(Campanula carpatica)*.

Edging is not necessary if your garden abuts paving stones or gravel, but if it meets the lawn, you have a problem. Edging may be a cinch with one of the new tools one sees advertised, but most of us are still cutting a clean line with hand shears and a trowel. Some

Matricaria 'Santana'

*. . . most perennials remain
free of disease and insects
unless they are unhappy
about their situations.*

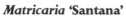

people try to avoid this job by sinking barriers of various kinds into the ground – stones, bricks, or those loathsome metal or plastic strips. Bricks laid flat and sunk deep enough that the mower wheels can run on them might work well (at least until the grass dives under them and comes up the other side), but anything that rises above lawn level must simply be trimmed *around,* which is more difficult than having nothing there at all. A clean line at the edge of a flower garden is most satisfying but is indeed troublesome to retain, since not only does the grass intrude on the garden but the perennials also tend to billow over the edge onto the lawn. Our highest authority, Miss Jekyll, considered this flopping good and proper, since it kept the garden from looking too hard and rigid. (The dictum would be particularly applicable to gardens of strict geometric design.) She spoke severely of the "tyranny of the turf edge." She admitted that the draped plants gave some trouble at mowing time:

> *When masses of foliage . . . hang over the grass it is difficult to mow to the edge. . . . But . . . this is just one of the points that makes a difference between the best and most careful and thoughtful gardening and gardening that is ease-loving and commonplace. **

Her solution to the mowing problem was to have a boy holding a bean pole moving backwards, lifting up the foliage of the floppers as he went, and a man advancing with a scythe, cutting the grass under the lifted foliage. "There is nothing in it," wrote Miss Jekyll, "that the plainest labourer cannot understand, while the added refinement that is secured is a distinct gain to the garden."

Lacking both the boy with the beanpole and the man with the scythe, I make shift by jamming in little stakes to hold the floppers out

---

* Jekyll, Gertrude, *Wall and Water Gardens.* New York: Charles Scribner's Sons (1901).

of the way temporarily while I mow, and I hope, when I've finished, that my garden has gained in refinement.

Gardeners are divided when they come to dealing with insects and diseases: two extremes, plus an inhabited area in-between. Organic gardeners use soap sprays, companion planting, and other benign methods of coping with infestations; they refuse to add to the pollution of the earth by spraying or dusting with noxious chemicals. The nonorganic gardeners spray away constantly and lightheartedly, taking an after-me-the-deluge approach. The people in between spray with chemicals only when they are desperate—and feel guilty about it. Luckily, most well-sited, well-nourished perennials don't need spraying. Mildew on delphinium, phlox, and bee balm can be handled if you dust them with plain sulfur (although Funginex works better), and one has only to struggle with one's conscience over the way to protect columbines from green worms and leaf miner, delphinium from cyclamen mites, and chrysanthemums (including shasta daisies) from their many diseases and flying enemies. But actually, most perennials remain free of disease and insects unless they are unhappy about their situations.

As to nourishment for your plants, if your soil was properly prepared—that is, if it was dug to a depth of twelve to eighteen inches and had peat and old manure or organic fertilizer added to it before the perennials were planted—you need merely make sure you are returning organic matter to the area fairly often. Consider how much of it is removed every year in the form of cut-back perennials.

The best fertilizer for hungry perennials is old cow manure; lacking that, use any other kind of well-rotted manure. If dollops are deposited near the greediest plants every fall or spring, no other fertilizer will be needed. Bone meal, compost, or other slow-acting organic material can be dug around the plants each spring. Some plants, of course, like a lean diet and shouldn't be fertilized at all. Again, they're the natives of rocky cliffs or sparse Mediterranean hills—red valerian, lavender, the mat-forming dianthus, some yarrows.

You will divide some of your plants every few years, and the necessary digging will aerate the soil. Certain perennials prefer never to be divided, some benefit from division every three or four years, and a few, such as chrysanthemums and dwarf asters, give of their best if divided every year. It isn't really an onerous task and can usually be put off until a convenient moment arrives. In cold climates, however, division of most plants is better done in spring, summer, or very early fall. Putting it off until late fall doesn't give the newly set roots time to get a firm grip on the earth before the freeze–thaw–heave process begins.

Aquilegia, platycodon, dictamnus, and gypsophila are some of the perennials that form taproots so want to be neither divided nor moved. But many others not only want but even require division now and then. You may ask yourself, why? It doesn't seem reasonable that a plant should need human intervention to do well, but since we have intervened to create many of our garden cultivars, we may be responsible for that need—certainly in the case of chrysanthemums and asters and no doubt in many others. They need dividing because the center becomes woody and weak, or the many divisions begin to choke one another.

Some plants (I am thinking now of primulas, but there are others) tend to deplete the soil they're growing in and become weak for that reason as well as from the choked condition of the clumps. They should be lifted, separated, and set into rich new soil. In nature, plants of this sort probably keep on the move, the mother plants dying and new seedlings coming up in a different place. There is another category of plants—those that do very well without being divided as long as they're fed but that one may want to divide in order to have more of them. Astilbes, Oriental poppies, peonies, Siberian iris, and geraniums are in this group. Yet another occasion for lifting and dividing perennials is when they've gotten too big for their spot and are crowding their neighbors.

Beginning gardeners are often terrified by the idea of dividing plants. New helpers in the nursery who are assigned the task look like young mothers who are bathing their babies for the first time, so afraid are they of doing irreparable damage. The fact is that plants, like babies, are pretty tough and are usually determined to live. However, while some of them—plants, that is—show you the way by obligingly separating themselves into neat, rooted pieces as soon as you begin wiggling them back and forth, others don't know what's good for them and stubbornly refuse to come apart. You must in this case keep cool, both physically and emotionally. Settle yourself in the shade with the proper tools and find some opening in the clump (there's bound to be one). You may help it to open by clipping down in the center with your pruning shears. Some plants can be pried apart with two garden handforks back to back. If that fails, I resort to an enormous steel kitchen knife, which I plunge into the opening and pound with a round wooden mallet my husband made from the knot of a tree. Once you've cut the plant in half, the worst of the battle is over; you go on from there, dividing the divisions, making sure each has plenty of root. Put them all in plastic bags immediately—don't let them dry out—and plant them as soon as possible.

Finally, there is the chore of staking. The way to avoid it is not to plant anything that needs it. Trouble is, you might end up with a boring landscape of mats and hummocks and no drama. Adrian Bloom, the English nurseryman, solves the staking question by making gardens of heather and variously shaped evergreens. His father, Alan Bloom, found a solution in island beds. He swears that even tall perennials planted in island beds in an open area without a background of hedge, wall, or building will grow so stout and strong they'll hold themselves and each other up. I haven't tried it, but I wonder if the winds at Bressingham Gardens are anything like the winds on this North American hill of mine. Other British gardeners use pea sticks (short, shrubby branches) or brush jammed in among the flowers to hold them up invisibly. They are invisible, all right, when the plants are burgeoning in June and later, but they look pretty dreadful all spring. I've been using slim poles from our woods, two or three to a plant, wound round with a soft yarny twine. Circular metal plant supports are also now available.

It's an irritating task, staking, no matter what system one uses, and one is grateful to subjects that provide height but take the responsibility themselves of remaining upright. Lythrum never keels over and looks like a big pink candelabrum into late summer. Trollius takes care of itself, as do daylilies, of course, and some of the latter, such as 'Hyperion', may rise to four or five feet. Goatsbeard makes a tall stout shrub all in one season. And let us not forget to be thankful for cimicifuga, large Solomon's seal, Japanese and *vitifolia* anemones, *Astilbe* 'Prof. van der Weilen', and Japanese iris. Barring a hurricane, amsonia of the gray-blue stars stands upright with no help, as do the big yarrows and *Dictamnus (fraxinella)*. Some say that globe thistle (echinops) has to be propped up, but not in my experience. *Filipendula rubra* 'Venusta', the queen of the prairie, grows to six feet and waves its great frothy pink heads triumphantly in the wind, asking for no assistance. *Boltonia* 'Snowbank' will provide you with a three- or four-foot foam of tiny white daisies for many weeks, late summer and fall.

In any case, the failure of some plants to stand without support may not be genetic. If a plant is growing in depleted soil or not getting the amount of water or light it needs, it tends to be wispy, lax, and unenthusiastic. Plants that are leaning desperately toward the sun are already half-prone before a storm knocks them flat. Some flop when they become congested. *Salvia nemorosa,* for example, begins to drape itself over its neighbors only when it has not been divided for a long time. Veronicas, the early true-blue ones (*V. teucrium* 'Royal Blue' and 'Crater Lake'), never grow straight up, but they try harder if frequently divided. So the moral of these observations is that if you keep your plants in the best condition, you may save yourself some work.

LEFT: Tiny white Campanula cochleariifolia *blossoms consort with the crimson cups of* Callirhoe involucrata. *BELOW LEFT: Early true-blue* Veronica *'Crater Lake' gives value to Iceland poppies, red valerian, and dianthus.*

ABOVE: The impact comes from setting dianthus against red-violet Salvia nemorosa. *Grays take the heat off. At the right, white* Papaver anomalum. *LEFT: The seed heads of nonclimbing* Clematis integrifolia *are almost as pretty as its nodding blue flowers. Underneath is the pink, cream, and green* Ajuga *'Burgundy Lace.'*

LEFT: *Iceland poppies often self-seed, making a colony that will last for years and bloom spring and fall. They hate hot weather, though, and often die in August.* BELOW: *Pinks, painted daisies, campanulas, and yarrow get a head start on delphiniums.*

LOIS O'CONNOR

GEORGE SHELDON

CONSTANCE SHELDON

The moment we wait for all year: everything looks glorious. Delphinium and goatsbeard back up the other explosions of color.

ABOVE: Painted daisies, or pyrethrum, are disease- and insect-proof, need only an occasional staking, and grow easily from seed. They come in luscious colors, too, both single and double. RIGHT: Fili-pendula venusta 'Rubra'. What could be better for the back of the border? Given sufficient moisture and light, it will carry your garden tri-umphantly through the hottest part of the summer. "Queen of the prairie," indeed.

BELOW: Rosa 'Donald Prior' glows among the silvers of artemisias and lavender. Double white feverfews spread themselves around, as do the tall, double pink poppies.

GEORGE SHELDON

CONSTANCE SHELDON

LOIS O'CONNOR

ABOVE: Light on the garden before a storm. *LEFT:* Delphiniums looking regal despite my rustic stakes. This perfection is fleeting: after the storm their appearance will not be quite so dignified.

11

CAMPANULAS

HAVING LONG FELT out of step with a culture in which "wild," "crazy," and "outrageous" are terms of praise, where discipline and restraint are qualities one tries to eradicate rather than cultivate, where even in the gardening world a jarring impact is preferred to subtle harmonies and a flower is advertised with pride as being clearly visible from 100 yards away, I was greatly solaced when I read Liberty Hyde Bailey's introduction to his book *The Garden of Bellflowers*.*

> *The bellflowers appeal . . . to the quieter and restrained emotions. Most of the species are not impertinent and gaudy, nor do they lend themselves to display. . . . They are eminently plants for the garden-lover, for those persons who . . . respond to the milder sensations and derive sustaining satisfactions from gentle experiences.*

It is surely true that with the possible exception of the newer

---

*Bailey, Liberty Hyde, *The Garden of Bellflowers*. New York: Macmillan (1953).

Campanula persicifolia

. . . tall, almost leafless stems rise to two or three feet, carrying clusters of white or lavender bells close to the stem that stand straight out or look up at you.

Canterbury bells, most campanulas are charming rather than impos-
ing, modest rather than flashy. They come in white, pale pink, and
shades of lavender and purple (invariably referred to as blue in the
catalogs), and to appreciate their color and form, close observation is
required for many of them.

Mr. Bailey gives another reason for his love of bellflowers:

> *They are not hopelessly confused by hybridization. [There] is
> now a persistent effort to cross everything that is crossable
> until original lines of singularity are lost, and the natural and
> distinctive marks of separation have no meaning. This abun-
> dant trend is assumed to be a horticultural gain, as if color-
> blobs and size-creations are proper objectives; yet the signi-
> ficant distinctions that arose with the species, that express the
> furniture of the earth, and have maintained themselves
> through the revolving centuries, constitute in themselves one of
> the keen rewards of the discerning and sensitive gardener.*

It's a good thing Bailey isn't around now to see the latest in
snapdragons, petunias, columbines, and hollyhocks. Not everyone,
however, admires only baseball-size double blossoms in glow-in-the-
dark colors. Plenty of gardeners are interested in growing less strident
plants—campanulas, for instance.

The word *campanula* comes from the Latin for "bell"—*campana*.
Of the family called Campanulaceae, or bellflowers, which includes
adenophora, symphyandra, and several others, campanula is the largest genus, having over 300 species. I find after making a list that I
have grown twenty of them myself, succeeding with some, failing with
others. The tricky ones are mostly the appealing little individuals
from the high mountains who hate hot humid weather and clay soil.
I've learned at least to get them up high in a gritty mixture, but even
that won't always satisfy them.

Most campanulas for the ordinary flower border are not at all
demanding after you have given them decent soil and good drainage.

They don't concern themselves with the lime/acid question and don't need rich food. And campanulas in general have the great virtue of being almost immune to disease and damage from insects.

You can buy seed for many of the good campanulas or get them through seed exchanges. Once you have them going, many kinds seed themselves, or the seed can be gathered and sown in flats. It's best to gather it as soon as it's ripe and sow it immediately. If you plant your flats late, they can be wintered over, the seed germinating in spring. Campanula seeds are usually as fine as dust and should be simply pressed into your moist but not soggy sowing mixture. They need light to germinate, so don't cover them with soil or put them in a dark place. The species should come true to type—only rarely do campanulas intermarry in the garden.

You can divide many of the plants rather than gathering seed, and in the case of hybrids or special forms, you may want to take cuttings. If so, take soft cuttings in the spring from unripe nonflowering or budding shoots. If the stems are hard, they won't root. Plunge them into sandy soil out of the sun, and cover them with cloches or even peanut butter jars. Whatever will keep your cuttings close but will let in the light.

Campanula persicifolia, the so-called peach-leaved bellflower, is probably the most widely grown. Its rosettes of long, smooth, narrow leaves spread by thin underground stolons to form a mat. From this, tall, almost leafless stems rise to two or three feet, carrying clusters of white or lavender bells close to the stem that stand straight out or look up at you. They are very lovely when they first open, especially the white ones, but as the individual flowers close their appearance detracts from the effect of the blossoms that are opening. If you have time and energy enough to deadhead, you don't have this annoyance, but busier or lazier people have to wait until the percentage of shriveled bells is greater than that of the opening ones and bravely cut back all the stems to several inches above the basal mat. The plants will then rise up and flower again cleanly. While we are mentioning faults, I must add that because this invaluable plant tips over during a storm, it must be loosely staked—*before* the storm. It also seeds itself with no thought of the rights of others, a regrettable characteristic. Still, I wouldn't be without. One must put up with a certain number of flaws in everyone. "New Giant Hybrids" of the species are offered by Thompson & Morgan, and several other older cultivars exist, among which 'Telham Beauty' comes in pale lavender blue. Double versions of both white and "blue" are offered by a few nurseries, but they seem to be not so tough as the singles.

Another common border campanula is *C. glomerata,* which comes in a deep rich purple and in white. In *glomerata* tight clusters of bells with pointed petals make little bouquets on top of one-and-a-half-foot to two-foot stems, emerging all down the stems as well as from the leaf axils. The basal leaves are long, rough, and somewhat hairy, not terribly attractive, but the flowers, especially in such cultivars as 'Joan Elliott', are of a hue that is stunning next to the pure blue *Delphinium* 'Bellamosum'. *C.g. dahurica* is also a particularly good form if you can find it. These campanulas don't seed themselves but spread fairly fast, running freely at the root, as one writer puts it. They should be shored up by pea sticks (short, shrubby branches) to keep them more or less erect. The white form, 'Crown of Snow', is about eight inches shorter than the purple one and blooms later and longer. *C.g. acaulis* is available both as seeds and plants. It has the same up-facing clusters of bells, of a paler purple or in white, and grows only a few inches high.

The English grow *Campanula lactiflora* (with milk-white flowers) extensively and consider it the best border campanula. They use both the species and several cultivars that seem to be little known in America. I raised about two dozen plants from seed one year. They flowered the following year and died to a man during their second winter. Since *C. lactiflora* is from the Caucasus and is listed for zone 4, I can't understand its behavior unless the drainage was at fault. I mean to try again, putting it in a better spot. Perhaps it can't take hot weather. It does seem odd, though, that it isn't used more in the United States. I can find it listed in only two of the plant catalogs in my bulky collection.

The explanation may lie in its cultivation requirements, as it doesn't transplant easily due to its thick, fleshy root. H. C. Crook, who knows everything there is to know about bellflowers, says the best method of growing it is to sow the seed *in situ,* thinning out the plants rather than transplanting them. After that there will be self-sown seedlings. Transplanting is possible, but individuals that have been moved take several years to recuperate from their apparently traumatic experience and may never attain the glory of their un-moved siblings, which produce great panicles of bluish white bells on strong straight stems. (Now I see that Wyman says *C. lactiflora* is "easily grown and easily propagated by division." There you are—when do two authorities agree?) There is a pale pink *lactiflora* called 'Loddon Anna'; a violet-blue one, 'Prichard's Variety'; and the eighteen-inch 'Pouffe', which has been impressing American visitors to English gardens recently. This species will tolerate a certain amount of shade.

I must admit to defeat with another tall campanula—*latifolia,* which is considered a good old garden workhorse by most authorities. One is warned to take care lest it spread unduly and told that since it's rather coarse, it might be naturalized in the wild garden. Nobody says a word about what it does in my garden, which is simply to disappear definitively after it finishes flowering. I've tried home-grown seedlings and imports named 'Brantwood' (red violet), 'Alba' (white), and the variety *macrantha.* If you can grow it—and apparently it's not easy to kill—you will enjoy its racemes of elongated, up-facing bells on the ends of four-foot stems that don't need staking. They rise from a clump of toothed, cordate, ovate leaves five to six inches long. *Latifolia* is native all the way from northern Britain east to Siberia.

Another campanula that is really a candidate for the wild garden is *C. alliariifolia.* I thought it would be splendid when I planted the seeds and coddled the growing babies, so was somewhat vexed when in the second year, three-foot stems surged up from the tufts of large, hairy, serrate leaves to produce, triumphantly, a number of long, tubular, nondescript whitish one-inch bells on a one-sided raceme. If you were to find it growing out in a field, you might be thrilled. I have a friend who even likes it in his garden. Crook says its seed "provides a ready (often too ready) means of increase."

Another one I grew and couldn't rouse any enthusiasm for was *C. punctata*. A conversation piece, perhaps; a successful border plant, no. It had long pointed, toothed leaves and sent its flower stems up to one and a half feet. From these drooped two-inch-long, very sad looking bells of dirty white to grayish purple, looking too big for the plant. Inside they did have interesting spots—of purplish maroon, as I recall—but without lying flat on your back in the border, which really isn't practicable, you couldn't observe them. *C. punctata* is, I understand, a great favorite with the Chinese and was introduced into the West from their country in 1844, to the delight of gardeners whose tastes I do not share. It has, however, been used as one parent of several first-class border plants.

Out in the nursery there is a batch of young *C. primulaefolia* plants that are due to flower for the first time next spring. The rosettes of long, crimped leaves really do look like those of a primrose, and this bellflower shares the primrose's fondness for damp, shady places. It is a native of Spain and Portugal so may or may not prove to be hardy here, but if it is, it will grow to three feet and carry lots of lavender-blue cups with a white center. The stems branch at the base only, thus producing a pyramidal effect.

Campanula carpatica is a rock plant that can be successfully used in the front of the border. Both the species and its many special cultivars are easily available and widely planted. If *carpatica* is divided every year, it remains a neat little dome of crinkled, heart-shaped leaves, usually no more than eight to ten inches high. It covers itself with half-open bells of lavender or white, beginning early in July and going on for a couple of months if deadheaded. The form *C.c. turbinata* is especially fine, as are 'Wedgwood Blue', 'Wedgwood White', and 'China Doll', all of which have very flat starry flowers. 'China Doll' is of an especially delicious color—palest lilac gray. There is a new mixed color strain of *C. carpatica* called, unfortunately, 'Jingle Bells', that is excellent; the plants are tight, tough, and floriferous.

There are several more rock campanulas that are both pretty and easy to please. *C. garganica,* a variety of *C. elatines,* is the best of these obliging ones and should be grown in a raised bed or retaining wall, where it will flatten its tiny ivy-shaped leaves against the rocks and send out long trailing stems in the crevices. When it blooms, in May, you won't be able to see the foliage for the hundreds of little blue-gray, white-centered stars.

Campanula portenschlagiana (muralis) is almost as lovely and certainly as easygoing. Its rounded, heart-shaped leaves are similar to those of *garganica,* though not quite so deeply incised, and it has the same growth habits and requirements. Masses of one-inch-long, erect lavender bells will appear on it in June and July.

C. poscharskyana is not so refined as the last two trailers but is vigorous enough to survive in the border as well as on a rock wall, where it really prefers to be. It has been known to run underground and come up in the territory of its less aggressive neighbors, so be forewarned. This species also has round, heart-shaped leaves with deeply serrate margins; they are on long footstalks and are much larger than the leaves of the other two. The flowers are slim, lavender-blue, half-inch to one-inch bells that appear in June and July. Grown next to a small shrub—*Potentilla* 'Abbotswood', for example—it could ramble and look good while doing no harm. It will grow well in full sun but rather likes light shade.

Campanula cochleariifolia (pusilla) is so tiny and dainty that one would think it difficult to raise. On the contrary, it's difficult to suppress. I've had a white one in the front of the border for years, where it behaves, but as soon as I put a piece of it up on a raised stone bed, it began to travel, fast. Now it's cheekily popping up into all the aethionemas, achilleas, armerias, and helianthemums that surround it. It has even sent its roots downward so they can poke their rosettes of shiny, oval, heart-shaped leaves out between the wall rocks. The miniature white bells look most beguiling, and I'm all for encouraging its spirit of enterprise except when it leads to smothering the neighbors. The bells are usually as wide as they are long and are known in England as fairies' thimbles. There are two named varieties of the blue *cochleariifolia* that I know of—'Miranda' and 'Miss Willmott'. They are charming, but I love 'Alba' the best.

Campanula raddeana is another underground spreader whose showers of gleaming deep-violet bells make it a plant to be treasured despite its pushy ways. On my wall it's beginning to cross swords with *cochleariifolia*. It comes from the Transcaucasian Alps so appreciates a high, well-drained stony spot. Obviously it can be propagated by division, but the seeds germinate readily.

There is a whole nation of small alpine campanulas. After poring over their photographs and descriptions one would like to grow each one, only to be given pause by the information that *this* one is a true alpine. A dazzling account of *C. cenisia* at home on the edge of glacial torrents in the high Alps continues "The best hope of success in cultivation rests in planting quite young seedlings in a non-limy, very loose scree, keeping them nearly dry in winter and providing a constant supply of underground water throughout the growing season." One simply can't have everything one wants. If I could just grow *C. raineri* of the "ash-grey foliage and erect large lilac bells," I might be contented, but since it wants a limestone crevice in a scree, I believe I'll pass on *C. raineri*.

The experts, as we have seen, don't always agree. Walter Kolaga says *C. pilosa* from Alaska is beautiful and easy in well drained soil in sun or light shade. Foster says it's *not* easy and may sit for years without blooming. It wants a fairly rich neutral soil and a site that is not too hot. L. H. Bailey says *C. alpina* has thriven in Ithaca, N.Y., blooming in late May and early June. Crook says it generally dies after flowering but that since it sets a lot of seed, you can grow it as a biennial. According to Foster, it seems less willing to bloom than most, and if you put it in a sunny, gritty spot, it will probably shrivel away. Putting it in richer soil in shade will produce a lush rosette, but it won't bloom. "When finally persuaded to flower it is apt to die of exhaustion." If you want to be sure, you have to try one that everybody agrees is easy.

I'm ordering seeds of *C. collina* because it's from the Caucasus, because the catalog says it has "semi-pendant bells of rich purple

blue," and because Farrer thought it gorgeous. And nobody says it has to have ice water running under its roots in August. I'm also going to try *C. fenestrellata* because it's closely allied to *C. garganica* and so might not be too temperamental. *C. barbata* sounds possible—that's on my seed list, too. I'd love to try *allionii* but don't dare. "From small

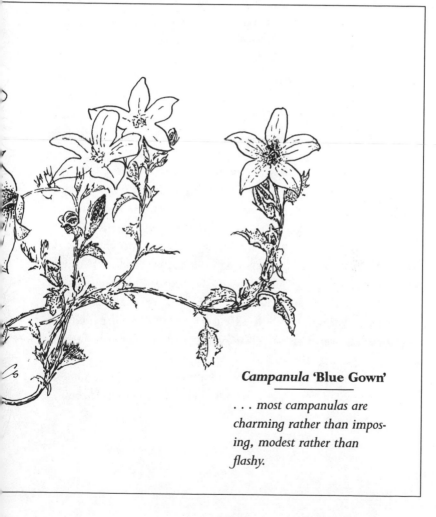

Campanula 'Blue Gown'

. . . most campanulas are charming rather than impos-ing, modest rather than flashy.

rosettes of narrow lanceolate leaves rise 1-2" stems carrying one or two large Canterbury bells," says the catalog. Oh dear—another scree plant.

I have scarcely mentioned *C. medium,* the real Canterbury bells. Although they are sometimes listed as perennials, they are certainly biennials and must be planted every year. The newer ones are mighty impressive but take up a four-foot pyramidal space in the flower border. There are some dwarf ones now that are fifteen to twenty inches tall. These come in white and shades of pink and so-called blue. Both single and double Canterbury bells are available, the singles being preferable to my mind.

Nor have I mentioned three other common bellflowers. The first, *C. rapunculus,* or rampion, has tuberous roots that have been much used as food in Britain and Europe, where it grows wild. *C. rapunculoides* grows wild everywhere, apparently, including the United States. It looks like adenophora, growing to two feet with long slender lavender, funnel-shaped flowers hanging along the stems. It is so pretty that some people make the mistake of putting it in their gardens, where this ruthless outlaw soon takes over all the available space by means of spreading roots and lots of viable seed.

C. rotundifolia is almost as persistent, but it does its colonizing by means of seed alone. You will be pulling it out by handfuls if you put it in your rock garden. This one is called Scottish harebells or blue-bells and grows on cliffs everywhere in the temperate zone. It has the peculiarity of having two kinds of leaves—round ones at its base and linear ones all over the rest of the plant. It makes masses of slender half-inch-long bells, lavender as a rule, but there is a white form.

I raised *Campanula scheuchzeri (linifolia)* from seed some years back. It resembled *rotundifolia* strongly but didn't seed itself about. A nice little plant. Try it.

12

AUGUST

AUGUST IS THE MONTH one spends dragging the hose around yet never managing to make up for the lack of rainfall. The sun blazes away relentlessly, day after day, while the radio announcers cheerfully predict another beautiful day—temperatures in the eighties or nineties. All radio announcers boat, swim, or golf in their leisure time. They hate cloudy days, and if there is some slight possibility of rain, they call it a "threat," even when all gardeners and farmers are on their knees praying for it. There is no moisture in the earth but lots of it in the air, and with the humidity around 98 percent, the situation is calculated to promote powdery mildew.

The perennial garden looks its worst in August except for the triumphant pink plumes of queen of the prairie (*Filipendula rubra* 'Venusta') . Almost everything else looks discouraged or in need of cutting back. There is a great gap where the delphiniums were, and they are only starting their new growth. What to do with the stakes? They look dreadful standing there, all bare and exposed, but without them the autumn delphinium spikes will fall over. Miss Jekyll said she planted white everlasting peas (*Lathyrus latifolius* 'Albus') behind them, then pulled the vines through to cover the cut-back delphiniums. But

Astilbe arendsii

. . . arranging things so that the garden looks good in August remains a problem.

G-S

if they are covered, how can they rise up to bloom again? And still there are those awful stakes . . . Columbines, which never care about their appearance after they've finished their lovely two-month-long display, are now full of yellow leaves and brown stems. Shastas are gone and are concentrating on the new green leaves at their feet. Painted daisies look as if they'll never pull themselves together for next year.

It's true that the phlox and daylilies carry on and the heleniums and helianthus look dramatic. By the end of the month balloon flowers are still producing a few of their elegant veined and pointed bells. And thank goodness for *Phlox* 'Miss Lingard', which frequently reblooms at this time, and for *Anaphalis triplinervis*, which saves itself for August and September. But the lawn is brown where it doesn't consist of ground ivy, and the astilbes are brown to match, all shriveled from lack of moisture. August is the month in which one would least like to receive a visiting garden club.

By September things look much better—with any luck we've had some rain and the Sahara winds have ceased. The lawn is green again and the asters are beautifully blooming, as are the Japanese anemones, the tall late sedums, and the chrysanthemums. Even the roses have taken heart and now venture to celebrate with a new flush of bloom.

But arranging things so that the garden looks good in August remains a problem. Nor have I learned how to avoid losing those plants that want sunshine but cool, dry air.

The unhappy situation can at least be ameliorated if there are in the garden plenty of plants with good foliage that love the heat yet can endure the cold. They could be so placed as to give the garden an appearance of thriftiness despite the presence of some bedraggled subjects that are just managing to survive. Dwarf shrubs, santolinas, *Achillea* 'Moonshine', artemisias, dianthus, thrift, the large sedums, nepetas, lavender—all these would answer the purpose.

As for the mountain plants, I have learned that they should not be put in full sun, even when that is their preference in their native habitat and in England. Morning sun but no afternoon sun seems to be better for these subjects. It is also helpful to place them so that they can get their roots under rocks, which will retain moisture in the soil and provide them with some protection from the heat. But what will protect them from the humidity, outside of an alpine house?

Last spring I raised from seed two dozen *Achillea clavennae*, a small gray-foliaged alpine, and very pleased I was to see them taking the morning sun, all stout little plants, happy in their pots of gritty soil. As the summer got hotter and more humid these small yarrows began to flag. I made sure they were not being attacked by insects and had enough water, then moved them to a cooler spot. They looked more and more miserable. By the end of August more than half of them were gone and the others looked almost hopeless—but lo! with the cool weather and dry air of September and October they revived and put out clean new growth.

Still, there is no pleasing some garden subjects. One year the entire summer was wet. Endlessly the water sluiced down, from late June through July and most of August. The hoses remained coiled against the house while we sloshed around in gumshoes between storms, spraying Funginex on the phlox and delphiniums, trying to ward off the mildew. Indoors the furniture and books, not having been sprayed with Funginex, broke out in white patches. My vetiveria plant, summering in the garden, must have felt that it was back home in India for the monsoons.

The last week of August produced, instead of rain, very cool sunny days with a dry wind. Our spirits rose even as we worked at trying to repair the rain damage. Lots of plants had been lost in the nursery, where the clay is heavy and the drainage is bad. We tilled, brought in new soil, and set about constructing ridges for new plantings. I took plants from the raised beds to replace the helianthemums and campanulas that had drowned in the border.

As I trudged back and forth, carrying on this flood repair work, I happened to glance at the astilbes. I had assumed they would still be happy as clams after having had over two months of their favorite weather. But I could scarcely believe what I saw—it was like a bad joke. After only ten days without rain the wretched things were brown.

13

DIANTHUS

Dianthus are marvelous plants, cheery and obliging, having next to no afflictions. There are types for both rock garden and flower border, all beautiful and nearly all deliciously fragrant. Most of them have attractive evergreen or glaucous foliage, which counts for a lot. Since no perennial blooms all summer (the claims of its vendors notwithstanding), a first-class plant must have handsome foliage both before and after blooming.

Among the many hundreds of species there are five principal classes of dianthus: *D. caryophyllus*, to which the carnation belongs; *D. plumarius*, a ten- to fifteen-inch tufted perennial; *D. barbatus*, or sweet william, which is grown mostly as a biennial; the very low mat-formers, such as *deltoides*, or maiden pink, and *D. gratianopolitanus (caesius)*, the cheddar pink; and the annuals, which come from *D. chinensis* or *D.c.* 'Heddewigii.'

Dianthus have been cherished in Europe for centuries and were featured in many paintings of the old masters, such as Holbein, Rembrandt, and van Eyck. Early settlers tenderly carried them to this country from their gardens at home. All varieties are referred to as pinks—not from their color, for they come in white, pink, rose, deep

Dianthus 'Essex Witch'

Dianthus will surely die under boggy conditions, although they can take a fairly heavy soil with drainage.

red, and even yellow, but from the crimped or pinked edges of their petals. *D. caryophyllus* was also called gilliflower or giliflour, gilliwer and gilofre, all corruptions of giroflée, from *girofle*, the French word for clove. Gilliflowers and *D. plumarius* were used in the Middle Ages to flavor wine, replacing the expensive cloves from India – which explains the name of one old cultivar still grown in England, 'Sops in Wine.'

Most people in the sixteenth and seventeenth centuries valued pinks not just for their beauty but also for their fragrance and included in their gardens only the scented varieties. Gerard, Parkinson, and most other early horticulturists did not grow the scentless species that we treasure in our rock gardens today – *D. alpinus, D. pavonius, D. sylvestris,* the yellow *D. knappii,* and the irrepressible *D. deltoides.* Neither would they have valued those countless brilliant annual pinks that are nearly all without scent.

The original species *D. caryophyllus* is a crimson flower, single and scented, that grows on limestone in southern France and northern Italy, frequently preferring rocky cliffs or old castle walls. Since it can be seen clinging to walls of Norman castles in England, too, at Dover and Cardiff, for example, it has been hazarded that its naturalization in England was one result of the Norman invasion. At any rate, horticulturists began to breed it at a fairly early date, so that by 1597 semidoubles were recorded, and in the 1600s Gerard mentioned, among others, a "Great Double Carnation" with three-inch flowers. It was found that when the flower was doubled the fragrance, too, was doubled. By 1650 two main sorts were listed – small, very fragrant clove gilliflowers with eighteen- to twenty-four-inch stems rising from a tuft of glaucous six-inch leaves, three to nine flowers on a stem, and tall, large-flowered carnations, the ancestors of our greenhouse varieties. In 1647 a book on the cultivation of *oillets* was published in Paris, the first book to be written on one flower. Hybridization went on apace, and a new book on the subject was printed a few years later. Parkinson's *Paradisi in Sole* devotes several pages to gilliflowers, the illustrations showing them to have been sumptuous and varied.

Dianthus plumarius, also referred to as grass pink and cottage pink, has been cultivated for as long as the clove gilliflower, but because it is not so tall and has smaller flowers it was less attractive to early breeders. In 1676 John Rea spoke disparagingly of grass pinks, but then he was a person who stressed beauty of form and color over fragrance – a forerunner of most of our plant breeders today. He thought the grass pink was good only as a filler in borders and bouquets. It was, however, valued highly as a medicine against fevers and as a heart remedy and was used in salads and confections as well.

D. plumarius, named by Gerard for its deeply fringed petals, also grows wild on limestone in Europe. The species has gray foliage, is five to fifteen inches tall, and has one to thirteen flowers in May and June. It is highly scented, especially the white variety, and often has a contrasting eye.

Of all the more recent developers of carnations and pinks, Montague Allwood of England is the best known. More than eighty years ago he crossed the perpetually flowering carnations with the grass pinks to produce ever-blooming hybrids, 'Perpetual Pinks'. They're a strong race with various color patterns, blooming from June until frost if they are suited.

In recent years so much hybridizing has gone on, so many crosses made between dianthus species and cultivars, that parentage of the plants now on the market would be difficult to ascertain.

In discussing the different classes of dianthus I will deal here in detail only with the perennials. *D. caryophyllus,* though listed as a perennial, must be treated as a biennial or a greenhouse plant in most parts of the United States. Hence I will give it short shrift.

For the front of the border, for use in rock gardens, or for sheeting down a wall, the mat formers are invaluable, especially in combination with little clumps of the small creeping or tufted campanulas, armerias, silenes, and helianthemums. *D. gratianopolitanus,* the cheddar pink (named for its native Cheddar Gorge in England), makes a three- to four-inch-thick blue-gray mat that is handsome even without the hundreds of single pale pink fragrant blossoms it bears, close to the mat, in May and June. It is almost indestructible and will spread to cover a three-foot area if allowed. There are several delightful cultivars of *D. gratianopolitanus* that are available, but they are not so dependable as the species. 'Tiny Rubies' is a cheddar pink congested into a small dense round cushion, which in spite of its name bears tiny pink flowers, not ruby red ones. Charming indeed, like a little hedgehog. 'Rose Cushion', 'Little Bobby', and 'Essex Witch' are no doubt also derived from cheddar pinks, being all smallish blue-green mounds with pink flowers.

Dianthus deltoides, the maiden pink, is a mat former with dark green foliage. The mat stays low, about three to four inches, but it carries its flowers on stems that rise four to fifteen inches high, small scentless flowers that are almost magenta red, very intense, or sometimes pink with a crimson eye. They also come in white with a pink inner circle. Trouble is, they seed themselves without stint and can become a pest if planted near timid, nonaggressive neighbors. There are several cultivars of this species that may be considered preferable, some of which also tend to seed themselves but with considerably less abandon. 'Flashing lights' is a good hot red, as are 'Fanal' and 'Brilliant' or 'Brilliancy'. 'Zing Rose', a beauty, has larger flowers than any of the above and makes a tuft, not a mat. It is advertised by the seed company that sells it as "blooming a few weeks after sowing . . . never stops all summer . . . performance repeated . . . year after year. . . ." Don't you believe it. 'Zing Rose' *is* a good plant but is not, at least in this area, to be relied upon to live through the winter.

Dianthus allwoodii 'Alpinus' forms large blue-gray mats like those of cheddar pinks except that they are a bit higher and looser. The scented single flowers come in shades of pink, white, red, and combinations of those colors, and the plant is just as tough and untemperamental as a cheddar pink. My favorite in this mixture is one that bears smoky rose-colored flowers with a dark red center. Very handsome. Though the cheddar pink blooms only once, in May and June, the *allwoodii* 'Alpinus' will usually rebloom if sheared immediately after flowering.

There are many marvelous species of these earth- or rock-hugging pinks, most of them easygoing, some of them refractory. I have grown here *D. arenarius,* with fine grassy leaves, white feathery flowers, and a faint scent; *D. pavonius (neglectus),* which sends up six-inch stems from a two-inch cushion and carries small deep-pink flowers that are buff-colored underneath; and *D. alpinus,* the prima donna of the family. It holds its glowing rose-pink blossoms close to its tight mat of broad, short, dark green foliage, and is, I admit, rather hard to please but worth any extra exertions it requires. Lincoln Foster says to give it plenty of light but not full sun. Another writer submits that it's more permanent in a moraine. Yet I've had a large healthy mat of it on level ground at the foot of a stone wall for many years. The offspring of this plant I move from place to place, trying to please them.

Dianthus plumarius grow to heights of fifteen to eighteen inches, usually in loose clumps of gray-green foliage. Their one fault is that they flop, especially after a rain, and must be guyed up with small stakes and a piece of gray yarny cord or propped up before it rains with pea sticks. The blossoms are fragrant and frequently double. There is a series called 'Spring Beauty' and an improved form called 'Sonata,' which I'm trying this year. The most glorious of all are 'Highland Hybrids,' recommended for underplanting old shrub roses.

Some of the loveliest *D. plumarius* are 'Laced Pinks', whose intricate patterns and color combinations were developed and prized by the Paisley weavers near Glasgow in the nineteenth century. Not to be confused with them despite the name are a 'Lace' series of dianthus that are marketed both as seeds and plants. These dianthus are derived from *D. superbus,* a tall plant with deeply fringed flowers ("lace" in this case meaning lacy; in 'Laced Pinks' the word refers to an embroidered design on fabric). The *D. superbus* 'Lace' series are listed as perennials but should be treated as biennials in severe climates.

Many named dianthus are forms of *D. plumarius* or crosses between *plumarius* and *caryophyllus*—salmon pink 'Helen' and 'Doris', white 'Aqua', deep red, very striking 'Warbonnet', and 'Oppenheimer's Red'. They are stunning plants both as to foliage and flowers but, alas, are not by any means so reliable in a rough climate as their less glamorous relatives. It's best to take cuttings to keep them going.

Other charming hybrids on the market are 'Sweet Memory', a ten-inch double white with a plummy red center, and 'Her Majesty', another ten-inch double white, no contrast. 'Spottii' is a three-inch red chubby little thing that is edged and spotted with white in such an ingenuous manner that it looks as if a child had drawn it with a crayon.

As for culture, all dianthus like a sandy, gritty soil containing lime, *D. pavonius* being one exception. It seems to prefer a soil that is neutral or slightly on the acid side.

Dianthus will certainly die under boggy conditions, although they can take a fairly heavy soil with proper drainage. Full sun or as close to it as possible is another requirement. One authority says that although all prefer full sun, they will grow in the shade of a building—but not with overhead shade. Apparently, they can tell when something is looming over them.

Even in sweet soil dianthus benefit from a yearly application of ground limestone and enjoy a mulch of limestone chips. *D. caryophyllus* and perpetually flowering pinks need a fat diet of either compost or 5-10-10 and wood ashes in early spring, but *D. plumarius* and the low species dianthus will thrive in poor soil as long as it's sweet.

Dianthus are said to do best where the extremes of temperature are not severe, but since they thrive here, where the extremes of temperature must approximate those of Inner Mongolia, I can only conclude that they are much more resilient than many horticulturists believe. In late November, however, I cover them lightly with pine boughs to cut the winter blasts.

Among the mat formers there is a tendency to become bare in the center. This problem can be obviated by top-dressing in spring and fall; that is, by sifting some loose sandy soil down through the middle of the rug. Another important task is to shear them of their flower stems and at least one third of their green or gray outer growth after they flower. (Don't forget to leave a small cluster of seed heads to mature if you want to gather seed). The plants will need to be cut back drastically in spring if they look shabby. When you cut off lots of the scraggly outer growth, you return the virtue of the plant to the center, and it will take on new life, burgeoning away and filling out into a nice neat tussock again. The loose *plumarius* types should be sheared, too, twice a year. They simply can't support all the growth that they recklessly put forth in their summer enthusiasm. You have to save them from themselves.

Since dianthus are not renowned for being long-lived, it is wise to try to produce one's own. The species dianthus come readily from seed, stout little plants popping up sometimes a week after sowing. It is better to sow perennials in flats than directly into the ground. Scrub your flats and sow seed in a commercially prepared sterile soil mixture to which perlite or fine gravel has been added. Put the flats in a warm, light, airy place. Keep them moist but don't overwater, especially after the tiny seedlings appear, lest they damp off. If you err, let it be in the direction of too little water rather than too much. Seed from the garden will no doubt have been mixed somewhat by the bees—some of your cheddars will be darker than others, for instance—but no matter, they are all lovely.

If you want to keep a strain pure, take cuttings right after flowering time, or in midsummer. Simply tear off a new side shoot with a bit of the main stem, or heel, attached. Remove the leaves at the lower end of the cutting, dip it in water and then in a rooting hormone, and insert it into holes in flats of peat and sand. Press in the cuttings, and keep the flats in a light but not sunny spot. (To preserve moisture I cover my cuttings with old meter covers discarded by the local gas and electric company. The covers make admirable cloches.) Cuttings taken in this way should root in about a month. The *plumarius* types can be divided in late summer, cut back, replanted deeply, and firmly pressed in. My impression is, however, that layering or taking cuttings is safer.

It's fun to experiment with different dianthus species. I'm growing *D. knappii* this year simply because it's yellow, although Foster calls it "an awkward plant." It comes from Hungary and Yugoslavia and has small half- to three-fourths-inch flowers, single or double, not fragrant. I had a nice pink dianthus for several years that I grew just for the name, 'La Bourbrille'. I'd love to try the 'Marguerite Carnations', which Hudson of the World Seed Service says will live for three to four years except where winters are severe. The Hudson catalog describes 'Malmaison Doubles' thus: "White, pale yellow, rose, pink, crimson, fringy petals, fine spicy scent, can flower within six months of sowing and will bloom until frost." Tempting, even if one's winters are severe.

In the last fifty years or so British gardeners have been trying to track down and salvage, for themselves and for future generations, the old cottage garden varieties of pinks. Some of them, at least, must have been available in this country in Louise Beebe Wilder's time, as she mentions, among others, the "blowsy but beloved 'Mrs. Sinkins'." It is no longer around, to my knowledge. How one would love to have the 'Earl of Carrick', a single fringed salmon pink, or 'Dad's Favourite', which English garden writer Margery Fish described as being "double white, heavily laced with chocolate and with a dark centre." Or the 'Crimson Clove' for its strong perfume; the 'Montrose Pink', mentioned in 1728; the 'Chelsea Pink', also called 'Little Old Lady', from 1760, described as "small, double, bright crimson, laced with white." There was one called 'Holbein', a 'Napoleon III', and even a 'Marie Antoinette'. Some of the old ones were mule pinks, apparently a sterile cross between sweet william and carnations.

Garden authorities list a host of plagues for dianthus–spider mites, thrips, wilt, stem and root rot, rust, leaf spot–but I must say, except for an occasional whitish spot on a gray leaf, I haven't, thank goodness, encountered any of these problems. Perhaps they attack mostly carnations. G. S. Thomas says that the "long periods of drying spring winds sap the strength of old plants." That's probably true; they sap the strength of everything else in the garden, including the gardener. But other enemies threaten pinks, as I once learned to my sorrow. There was in my garden the most delicious mat of cheddar pinks, seven or eight years old, tight and healthy, flourishing as if native to the place and never regretting the chalk cliffs of their homeland. Then, one spring when I lifted off the pine boughs that had been protecting them from the wind and the rabbits, I found a family of mice. They had tunneled here and there and chopped up the lovely foliage for nests. My beautiful cheddars – completely demolished, by mice.

14

PLANT NAMES

THERE'S NO DENYING IT: many of the proper, botanical names for plants are ugly. It does seem perverse to call a modest little plant with bright blue flowers *Ceratostigma plumbaginoides* (this is supposed to be an improvement on its former name, *Plumbago larpentiae*). Or consider *Anigozanthus manglesii* or *Elscholtzia dimorphotheca*. Some gardeners have felt very strongly indeed about botanical plant names. William Robinson, the great British horticulturist, fulminated against them, fortifying his arguments with such comments as, "Think of the British maiden or her mother struggling with such pedantic ugliness!"

Common names usually come from an attempt to describe a plant or indicate its uses, which is all, one would think, the average flower gardener would need in a name. The trouble is that people in different countries and often people in different regions of the same country have given well-known plants different names. What is a marigold to an Englishman is a calendula to us. What is a marigold to us is an African marigold to him. What is wild lily of the valley in one part of the United States is a Canadian mayflower in another. As for shrubs, Isabel Zucker in her book *Flowering Shrubs* lists the common names, which are dismayingly numerous, for each shrub she de-

Scabiosa caucasica

. . . *why don't they sit down
and think of a new name for
the lovely flower* scabiosa, *so
named because it was once
thought to cure that disgusting disease, scabies?*

GS

scribes. *Shepherdia argentea* is variously known as silver leaf, buffalo berry, rabbit berry, beef-suet tree, and wild oleaster. *Viburnum cassinoides* can be withe rod, swamp viburnum, swamp blackhaw, false Paraguay tea, wild raisin, Appalachian tea, or teaberry. The English hawthorn (*Crataegus monogyna*) can be called single-seed hawthorn, haw bush, hag-thorn, hagbush, hagtree, May bush, May bread, May bread-and-cheese tree or bush, aglet tree, fairy thorn, Glastonbury thorn, hipperty haw tree, holy innocents, heg peg bush, moon flower, peggall bush, pixie pear, quick thorn, scrab, scrab bush, or shiggy. All depends on where you're from.

Elizabeth Lawrence loved the "sweet country names" of flowers and shrubs, and Louise Beebe Wilder has a chapter on plant names in her 1918 book, *Colour in My Garden*. She was concerned lest the charming old familiar names of plants be lost and writes of them with great knowledge and affection, but even she, after discussing the custom of giving the same name to several different plants and many different names to the same plant (fifty-six names have been recorded for the marsh marigold, or *Caltha palustris*), admits that we must indeed learn the botanical names, cumbersome though some of them may be.

It seems the only possible solution for people who take plants seriously and want to talk or write about them, to buy them without ordering the same plant two or three times, to grow them – and to insist on knowing what is being offered in nursery catalogs. Any nurseryman who advertises "winterberry" should be made to say whether he's talking about *Ilex verticillata* or *Euonymus radicans erecta*, which share that common name but little else. Some of the less conscientious nurserymen even seem to be inventing "common" names for plants, to further confuse the situation. Many garden plants don't possess common names in English, since we use in our gardens today plants that come from all over the world, and if we knew what the natives back home called them, we wouldn't be much ahead.

The obvious conclusion is that we should familiarize ourselves with the botanical names as the only way out of the confusion. Many gardeners accept this logic but think themselves incapable of learning them. Actually, if you are really interested in plants, as you work with them and read about them their names lodge themselves in your head without much—sometimes without any—conscious effort.

Some people don't try to learn plant names because they think they couldn't pronounce them even if they could spell them. But the main thing is to be able to recognize the names in print—the pronunciation isn't terribly important. Of course, none of us like to make mistakes—we're afraid of sounding silly or ignorant. Never mind. It's like learning a foreign language: we've got to charge ahead and use the words we've learned even if we say them wrong, or we'll never speak the language. Besides, even the authorities disagree on pronunciation.

Nowadays horticultural magazines, reference books, and even plant and seed catalogs usually indicate the "proper" pronunciation of botanical names. This guidance is helpful—especially when the several sources are in accord. In many cases pronunciation is a matter of personal preference. Do you say STOKES-ee-uh because stokesia was named for a chap called Stokes or sto-KEES-ee-uh? Do you prefer DAHL-ee-uh or DALE-ee-uh? If you say SY-klam-en and I say SIK-lam-en, if you say klem-AH-tis and I say KLEM-ah-tis, it is not a matter of great moment. When syllables are inserted gratuitously, however, it *is* a bit irritating: gypsophila really *must* be jip-SOFF-ill-a, not jip-so-FILL-ee-a.

My bible on this subject is A. W. Smith's *A Gardener's Book of Plant Names*, which I hear is about to come back in print after a long period off the shelves. It's a charming, easy-to-read reference that explains the whole system of plant classification and nomenclature and offers, here and there, amusing anecdotal material. When you look up halesia, the silver bell tree, you'll learn that it was named for the Reverend Stephen Hales (1677–1761), who not only contributed to our knowledge of plant pathology but also invented a method of ventilating prisons to control jail fever and ships to prevent dry rot, developed a solution to the problem of weevils in stored wheat, and one Sunday morning, with the cooperation of a white mare, carried out what may have been the very first measurement of blood pressure. One wonders why he wasn't delivering a sermon instead.

Col. Smith says that the first classification of plants, that of family groups, is of more interest to botanists than to ordinary gardeners, as the family name is not included in the name of an individual plant. The names that are important to us are those of a plant's genus and species. Campanula, a genus that includes around 300 species of bellflowers, can be a four-foot back-of-the-border plant, a tiny rock-garden creature no bigger than a pin cushion, or one of many individuals of sizes, shapes, habits, and preferences in-between. If you don't know that *Campanula medium* is a three- to four-foot-tall biennial, and *Campanula tommasiniana* is a three- to four-inch rock garden perennial, you're going to have trouble.

Some of the genus and species names are in Latin and Greek, and some are in a sort of fake Latin—latinized names of people, places, and so on. Some species names contain information about the plant, such as its color, shape, size, or place of origin. If you learn some of the meanings of plant names, it helps you to remember them and to recognize the plants. Thus, *albus* means white, *hirsutus,* hairy, *glaucus,* having a white powdery coating or bloom. *Macro* is large or long; *phyllus* has to do with leaves. The species name *glaucophyllus* tells you that the plant has gray or bluish green leaves. *Macrophyllus* indicates that its leaves are large or long.

When the species names reveal places of origin, such as *pratensis,* from the fields, *montanus,* of the mountains, *saxatilis,* found among rocks, or *palustris,* swamp loving, you are immediately instructed as to the site preference of your plant. You'll put *Salvia pratensis* out in the open, *Myosotis palustris* in a wettish spot, *Alyssum montanum* and *Allium saxatile* on a rock wall. *Anemone sylvestris,* you'll know, wants a bit of shade, *sylvestris* meaning that it grows in the woods. Everything begins to make sense. Well, almost everything.

Most plants have only two names, that of the genus and that of the species, but some have three, either because they are distinct varities of a species or they are special garden cultivars. We have, for instance, *Aster* (genus) *alpinus* (species). Then we have a plant called *Aster alpinus garibaldii,* the last name indicating that it is a variety or subspecies of *Aster alpinus,* with enough differences to make it special but not enough to call it a separate species. *Aster alpinus* 'Dark Beauty', on the other hand, means that this form either has been produced by hand pollination of various alpine asters or is reproduced vegetatively from a special form of the aster that someone discovered or developed. Cultivar names are always capitalized and enclosed in single quotation marks except in catalogs or plant lists. These plants, as a rule, do not come true from seed but must be propagated vegetatively by means of cuttings, division, or layering. Cultivars can also be hybrids, which are sometimes but not always indicated by $\times$, as in *Achillea* $\times$ 'Moonshine'.

I will not go into the system of agreement in gender between species names and generic names, which may be masculine, feminine, or neuter. Col. Smith makes the crooked straight and the rough places plain in the introducton to his book; after you've read it, you'll know why a white gasplant is called: *Dictamnus albus* but a white gentian is *Gentiana alba.*

There is one thing about this business of plant names that doesn't make sense, and that is that the taxonomists are so often changing them. One assumes that they're not just amusing themselves, that it's all done in the interests of greater accuracy or to correct a faulty classification. But I know of at least one case where they've made things murkier instead of clearer—the case of French tarragon, which has been for many years *Artemisia dracunculus* or *A.d.* var. *sativa,* while the worthless "Russian" or Siberian tarragon was *Artemisia redowskii.* Then, a few years ago, the edict went out that they were both to be called *A. dracunculus. Hortus Third* says, cryptically, "variety *sativa* is listed." After years of trying to keep my herb customers straightened out, I felt pretty cross—still do, actually. Now all I can tell the novices is that if their plant (bought from somebody else, of course) sets seed, it's the Siberian interloper; they should chuck it out and get the one that has to be divided or grown from cuttings, since the good one is sterile.

Many other changes are almost as irritating, going from simple to difficult. *Dianthus caesius* changed to *D. gratianopolitanus* and *Campanula muralis* to *C. portenschlagiana. Clematis paniculata,* long the name of the sweet autumn clematis, seems to have become *C. maximowicziana,* of all the outrages, and *Chrysanthemum rubellum,* as in *C.r.* 'Clara Curtis', is suddenly *C. zwadskii latilobum* 'Clara Curtis'. Where are all these Slavs coming from? I've just discovered that *tunica,* which is pronounceable by all of us, has recently been rechristened *petrorhagia.* A big help.

If the taxonomists want a project, a really useful assignment, why don't they sit down and think of a new name for the lovely flower *scabiosa,* so named because it was once thought to cure that disgusting disease, scabies? And then they can move on to our poor native blue lobelia, which was also thought to cure an affliction and has thus been struggling along all these years burdened with the embarrassing name of *Lobelia siphilitica.*

15

VERONICAS

THE BEST WAY TO LEARN about something is either to promise to give a talk on it or to write about it. I've been growing veronicas for years without ever getting them properly sorted out, so I've decided that it's time to clarify matters.

Even now, however, after having scuffled through lots of books, seed lists, and descriptions, I find there are still some foggy areas when it comes to identifying the parentage of some of the garden cultivars. This obscurity is also true of many of the nonspecies garden plants—dianthus, salvias, and many more. Other misty areas occur where authorities can't agree on whether a plant is simply a variation of a species or a separate species, a distressing situation to those of us who want things to be neat and who like to make lists and charts. But, I tell myself, one shouldn't become as obsessed with organization as a linguist who was my supervisor when I was teaching English in Turkey. We were supposed to teach by means of speech patterns, for which he had made charts. When the language didn't fit, he jammed it in anyway, doing a sort of Procrustes job on it. That's going too far with a passion for neatness.

It is said that taxonomists are roughly divided into two sorts, the

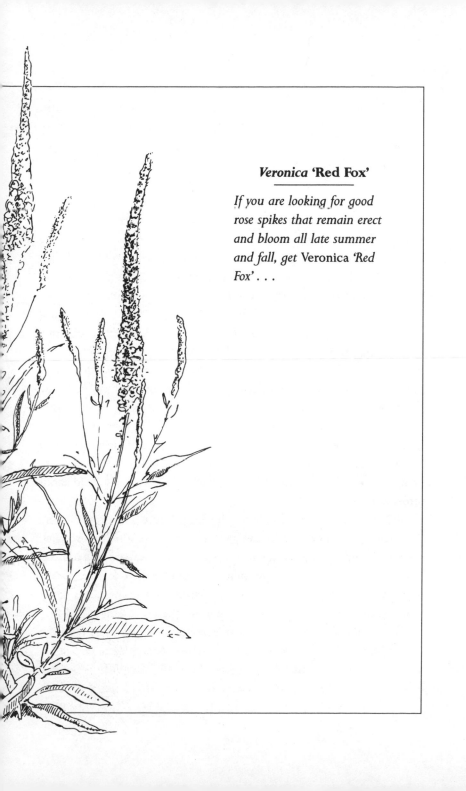

Veronica '**Red Fox**'

*If you are looking for good
rose spikes that remain erect
and bloom all late summer
and fall, get* Veronica 'Red
Fox' . . .

lumpers and the splitters, each group having its following. One person will say that *Campanula garganica* is a variety of *C. elatines*, whereas another will hold that it is "closely allied" but not the same species. We gardeners who are neither botanists nor taxonomists must stand apart from the fray, be as meticulous as possible, and simply record differences of opinion where they exist, although we may emotionally adhere to one opinion over another.

Take the case of *Veronica exaltata*, which is somewhat similar to *V. longifolia* and which Graham Thomas describes so lovingly and enticingly that one longs to get one's hands on it. He tells us it is a four-foot native of Siberia that blooms in late summer. "This most beautiful plant is far superior to *V. longifolia*, and as a rule stands well without staking. Jagged-edged leaves are arranged up the single stems, which each support a plume of clear and lovely light blue tiny flowers. Superb when grown near late astilbes . . ." Alan Bloom also gives it full marks, that is, 10 out of 10, for its four- to five-foot spikes that remain erect and bloom at such a convenient time of year. One rushes for one's catalogs. No *V. exaltata* anywhere. Next, Wyman. No *V. exaltata*—not a word. Finally, *Hortus Third*, who says "*V. exaltata: V. longifolia*," and doesn't mention it again. Even B. Harkness, in his *Seedlist Handbook*, says the two plants are the same. It's enough to make one bang one's head against the wall. What was that I said about remaining calmly on the sidelines?

But I haven't even given you the big picture of veronicas and the many roles they play in the garden. They are sometimes called speedwell and belong to the snapdragon family, or *Scrophulariaceae*. The mulleins (verbascum), penstemon, turtleheads (chelone), to say nothing of snapdragons, are among the better-known members of the same family. Veronicas have leaves that are paired or single and produce their small flowers singly or in spiky racemes that emerge from the leaf axils. The flowers are most often lavender, blue, or purple but may be had in white and shades of pink as well. The 250 species run from flat creepers to bushy plants five feet tall, as in *V. exaltata*, wherever it is. There are some shrubby New Zealand plants that were formerly classified as veronicas but are now listed with the hebes.

Veronica has gotten a bad name, at least in central New York, through the misbehavior of an individual called *V. filiformis*. Everyone has a story about how it started here – a Cornell botany professor triumphantly brought it back from foreign parts, or some such tale. It might be true; Cornell professors are always going to Asia Minor, which is the real home of *filiformis*. I must say it's taken enthusiastically to the gardens and lawns of this region – our climate doesn't upset it a bit. The plant grows only an inch or two high, has pretty little crimped leaves, and in spring spreads a mist of palest blue over Ithaca and now Lansing, since I unwittingly imported some on a gift plant from another Cornell professor. It's very pretty, actually, and one wouldn't mind it in the lawn at all if the green of its leaves were the same color as grass. Since it's a far lighter shade, it makes lawns look blotchy. Mowing only spreads it further; selective weed killers fertilize it. In the flower border it forms a delicate-looking but very tough net over all the earth and the other plants. So when I advise new gardeners to plant veronica, they recoil in horror, since *V. filiformis* is the only one they know about. It's difficult to persuade them that not all veronicas are gangsters.

Even the other creepers have their uses, although *V. prostrata (rupestris)* is a bit too fond of traveling to make a good subject for a small rock garden. The leaves of this plant are attractive, small, shiny, dark green, and toothed, and the flowers, while they are available in white and pink, are usually violet blue. It can be used on top of a large wall, in a spacious rock garden, or in the front of the border. A more delicate creeper is *V. repens*, which can be grown from seed and makes a lovely little mat, flowering most often in palest blue (not lavender) but sometimes in white, light pink, or a darker blue. Some writers say it can be used between stepping stones, on terraces, and for trailing in rock crevices. I have it on a wall and have found that with luck it will seed itself. This one needs encouragement rather than thwarting.

The really blue *Veronica pectinata* seems to be hard to find, either as seed or plants. Mine all comes from a plant a friend gave me long ago. It's another ground hugger from Asia Minor but is not at all aggressive. The leaves are toothed and downy—you will like it even before it blooms. The tiny racemes of flowers attain only about two inches; the corollas are deep blue with white centers. It is especially effective clambering over a large rock or sheeting down from a dry wall. *V. pectinata* 'Rosea', sold by many nurseries, is quaint and rather pretty, with pink and white flowers. Its foliage is furrier and grayer than that of the blue one.

In a raised bed in the nursery I have *Veronica armena* growing near the blue *pectinata*. The plants are very similar, both being low evergreen creepers with hairy, incised leaves. I went out to look at them carefully on March 8: They were forming terminal spikes of buds, getting ready to bloom. The temperature in the previous two days had been in the high sixties, so a bit of bright blue was already visible. Alas, the plants would have much fierce weather to undergo before spring really came! (The thermometer dropped fifty-seven degrees in the following twenty-four hours.) As I peered at the two plants I noticed for the first time that they both had two kinds of leaves. Some of the trailing stems on each plant carry quarter-inch single, lanceolate leaves—almost the shape of elongated diamonds—and others have the usual incised ones. In *armena* the incised leaves are deeply lobed and appear at the tips of the stems, almost like that of miniature palm leaves. The flowers of *armena* are nearly the same blue as those of *pectinata* but without the white base.

Veronica alpina is a good subject for either the front of the border or for a rock garden. I don't have the species of this six-inch shrublet, but since its lavender blossoms are described as evanescent, I won't bother to look for it. *V.a.* 'Alba', which I do have, blooms for weeks and weeks. Another small shrubby one that blooms forever is 'Heidekind', with dark green foliage and pudgy, deep rose spikes. It is six to eight inches high and will spread to a foot or more.

There are many rock garden veronicas other than the ones I grow, including several more creepers—*V. saturejoides,* from the Balkans, whose dense short racemes of deep blue flowers appear on three-inch stems in May and June, and *V. serpyllifolia,* thyme-leaved veronica, about which the authorities don't agree. A rock garden expert says it is "an improved *alpina* with better habit and larger, dark striped blue flowers," whereas Wyman says it's a native perennial weed, at its worst in lawns. *Hortus* says it's a naturalized import from Asia and Europe but says nothing about its being a pest. Dare one try it? Does one already have it, perhaps, in the weed collection in the lawn?

Everybody agrees that *Veronica fruticans (saxatilis)* is wonderful. It's another small shrub, this one with half-inch, closely set, dark green shining leaves. The "vivid royal-blue" flowers with red eyes sound equally alluring. It was on the American Rock Garden Society seed list this year—what a pity I didn't try to get it! I didn't know about *V. chamaedrys,* either, which is also called germander speedwell. Those who have grown it say it carries loose sprays of lovely bright blue flowers in May and June on a ten-inch spreading clump of crisp green, almost evergreen leaves. It's another import from Europe and Asia that has become naturalized here. Although one writer says it makes a good ground cover because of its compact habit and spreading rootstock, no one calls it a weed.

If I have been late in getting around to rock garden veronicas, I have been growing the border varieties with great pleasure. It would be difficult to have a good perennial garden without them, as most are long bloomers with, so far, no discernible diseases or enemies. They grow without complaint in any reasonably good garden soil and need division only every two or three years to keep them at their best. I would fault them on one thing, the slovenly posture of some of their spikes. I can't understand it—what's the use of having a lovely spangled spike of flowers if it's going to lie down on its back whenever it feels like it?

Some of the good border veronicas are species, but most of them are cultivars, often crosses between *V. longifolia* and *V. spicata* or sometimes derived from *V. latifolia* (Hungarian speedwell, also called

V. teucrium). The earliest to bloom in spring are the latter group. They are the only veronicas I know, outside of some of the rock garden species, that are truly blue. They are also, unfortunately, fleeting, blooming for no more than two weeks. Their twelve-inch stems are lax, so the blue spikes don't exactly stand up like soldiers, but the plant is well worth growing for its color. It is less floppy, of course, if it's divided regularly. I like it with the pale *Allium moly* or with *Euphorbia epithymoides (polychroma)*, which is sulfur yellow. Several versions of this plant exist, all of them much alike but graduating in intensity of blue in the order given: *V.t.* 'Shirley Blue', 'Crater Lake', and 'Royal Blue'. There's a nine-inch *latifolia* with golden foliage and light blue flowers called 'Trehane' that I've never seen and won't search for; I'm one of those people to whom yellow or golden foliage does not appeal. I always feel one should quickly dose it with iron chelate.

A gray-foliaged species from Asia that has everyone's vote but mine is *V. incana*. Although I love its low mat of three-inch silvery leaves, I've replaced it almost everywhere because its fine lavender spikes just won't stand up. I much prefer 'Saraband', probably a cross between *incana* and *spicata*, whose foliage is almost as gray as that of *incana* and whose racemes of deeper violet-blue flowers never collapse. It blooms from June until fall if the spent stems are removed. 'Minuet' is a smaller gray one (gray-green, really), only ten to fifteen inches, with pink flowers. It is not so sturdy a plant as 'Saraband' nor as upright.

If you are looking for good rose spikes that remain erect and bloom all late summer and fall, get *V.* 'Red Fox', a fine green-leaved *spicata* cultivar. It's a larger (ten to fifteen inches) version of little 'Heidekind'. There's also a 'Blue Fox', just as well-behaved.

Veronica 'Icicle' seems to be a *spicata* × *longifolia* hybrid. It is pure starry white and is the glory of the garden in years when it is so inclined, shooting up to around eighteen inches and looking almost as imposing as eremurus. Other years it dwindles and droops. Since I haven't solved the mystery yet, I put 'Icicles' here and there, trying to find the spot where they will finally be content.

Veronica longifolia, the species, usually grows about three feet tall, blooming from July to September. It has long jagged pointed leaves and often, but not always, remains erect. 'Blue Giant' or 'Giantess' is one for which seeds are sold. It has flowers of a not-very-distinguished lavender, but it is serviceable, making large upright clumps and pro viding a few seedling plants every year. 'Blue Peter' is a better, darker blue but is not as dependable. 'Sunny Border Blue', an eighteen- to twenty-inch dark violet-blue, is a splendid plant, sturdy, striking, and long blooming. The two-and-a-half-foot 'Foerster's Blue' sends up dark purply-blue spiky racemes for many weeks, sometimes not giving up until singed by frost.

I have one late summer veronica with glossy leathery leaves, that are perhaps five inches long, saw-toothed, and pointed. I got it as 'Blue Charm'—its species name is *V. grandis holophylla*—but it is a darkish lavender, not blue. 'Lavender Charm' is also offered in catalog—I wonder what color that one is?

My very favorite veronica, *V. gentianoides,* I have saved for the last. When I first raised this plant from seed, I naturally fancied it would be gentian blue. When it flowered the second year, I felt I had been robbed, for its straight little stems broke out into small veined flowers the color of skim milk. It turns out the *gentianoides* meant that it had leaves like those of certain gentians. But this unassuming plant gradually wins one over. It has a charm all its own and is shown at its best when grown against a dark background. It never allows its flower stems to collapse or even to lean over, and its rosettes of thick, smooth leaves are neat and satisfying to contemplate at any time. A variegated form of *V. gentianoides* exists.

It should be mentioned that *Veronicastrum virginicum,* Culver's or bowman's root, is often listed as *Veronica virginica.* It grows wild over much of North America, has six-inch-long narrow, toothed leaves in whorls and sends its racemes of small white flowers sometimes as high as seven feet. Storms do not knock it over, and I plan to make a little forest of it somewhere in my garden this summer. I hope it will look impressive through late summer, when the garden needs all the help it can get.

16

WINTER

Perhaps the first step in gardening is to accept the insuperable handicaps. When I lived in Virginia, I was happy to have the climate and acid soil that enabled me to grow tender azaleas, but I wrong-headedly kept trying to grow lilacs as well. If you live in Louisiana, you might as well face the fact that you can't grow alpines or any perennials that need a cold period every year and dislike heat and humidity—delphiniums, for example. In Michigan, Minnesota, or North Dakota you must decide you don't mind doing without camellias and the cold-sensitive rhododendrons. Those whose gardens are in the great central mass of the country sometimes feel they have the worst of it, since they have to prepare for extremes of heat in the summer, arctic cold in the winter, and worst of all, that yo-yo period in the spring when the thermometer may rise or fall forty-five degrees in twenty-four hours.

We are not spoiled in our part of the United States, either. We are told that there are fewer hours of sunshine here per year than anywhere else in the country. We have torrential rains in spring and fall and a Saharan drought in between. There is a good deal of mist at any season, and there are many gray days when absolutely nothing is

Spiraea 'Snow Mound'

*Molly the dog chases the deer
away during the day . . .
But they seem to know she's
inside at night and sneak
back into the garden to
browse on fruit trees and
shrubs.*

happening—no sun, no light, no rain, just a sort of limbo. Fierce winds often break off tree branches and flatten the flowers. We take comfort in reminding ourselves that we get no hurricanes or cyclones, only blizzards and hailstorms.

Still, whoever arranges the weather here does a very poor job of it. I've made my share of bitter remarks about the fortunate British and those lucky people in our Northwest (never mind that it rains there all the time—the plants like it). No wonder they have wonderful gardens. But we can't have it all. Whatever our climate, we *can* cultivate the old faithfuls of the region, then branch out, little by little, trying new things that might possibly make it. We sometimes surprise even ourselves.

The idea is to keep searching for plants that with a little help and encouragement can learn to tolerate and even enjoy life in the environment we provide. Don't give up too easily.

If you live in zone 4 and a plant you badly want is recommended for zone 5, don't let that keep you from attempting to grow it. I try borderline plants at least three times before throwing in the towel. If the plant you're experimenting with dies, try it again in a different spot. It may be that the soil didn't suit it, that the drainage wasn't good enough, that the site was too dry, too sunny, too shady, too acid, or too limy. Perhaps there was competition from neighboring plants. In short, it may not have been the temperature that did it in. Often we think a plant died of the cold when actually it drowned, or it was already so miserable that it didn't find it worthwhile to fight its way through the winter. Go back to the books, study the preferences of the individual you're dealing with, and do your best to satisfy it the second time around.

There are ways to mitigate the effect of a trying climate on garden plants, but it seems to be less difficult to fight the cold than the heat.

Garden literature often recommends siting a tender plant "in a protected spot." That may be advisable in some cases but not in others, for a plant can apparently be lulled into a false sense of security. Plants set in a cozy corner on the south side of a house are not only protected from the winds but also artificially warmed by sunlight reflecting off the building, especially if it's white. Thus they may think spring has come in February, start their juices flowing, and begin to open their buds, only to discover their mistake when the thermometer drops below zero again.

The practice of creating artificial microclimates by means of shrubs, trees, and buildings must be more consistently successful in milder climates than it seems to be here. Elizabeth Lawrence, who lived in North Carolina, wrote of "little sun-soaked enclosures" where angles of a house and cleverly placed shrubs made it possible to extend the flowering season considerably. Her plants were not subsequently damaged by a spell of severe cold.

When I was buying and planting some Japanese holly bushes, *Ilex crenata* 'Convexa', I consulted Isabel Zucker's *Flowering Shrubs*. They would survive the winter here, she said, and they would actually do better in the open. I didn't believe her, but it turns out she was absolutely right—the ones out in the border never lose a branch, whereas those huddled up against the house frequently have to be trimmed back past the dead wood.

Yet my Swedish neighbor, who was a wizard gardener, grew *figs* here by planting the tree against the south side of his house. His concessions to the climate consisted of pulling the fig tree down to the ground and covering it with a heavy mulch in late fall.

For me, too, the winterizing process starts in fall, when I make trips to local pine woods and bring back sacks of pine needles to put in thick layers around the azaleas, the rhododendrons, and other acid-loving evergreens. I begin to round up old baskets. I go to our back fields with wagon and saw and get red cedar trees, whose branches I put on the heath and any other delicate thing lest it be burned by cold winds. I make sure that all the evergreens are thoroughly watered before the ground freezes. (Around here, where the ground freezes, thaws, and freezes over and over all winter, I feel uneasy when I see the directions, "Mulch only after the ground freezes.") I get wheelbarrow loads of earth and mound up the bases of the roses. I put baskets and cloches over small tender things. I used to make burlap houses around my middle-sized rhododendrons and spray the big ones with antidesiccant, but they've been on their own for several years now. Collars of metal hardware cloth go around the bases of young trees in an attempt to protect them from rabbits and mice. Heavy paper tape can be used on the trees if it's available, but whichever you use, it should go up as high as three to four feet; rabbits seem to be perfectly comfortable standing on their hind legs, and when a crust forms on top of several feet of snow, they don't even have to go to the trouble.

My husband and I work together putting up the antideer devices around the young trees. It's exasperating work at best, stumping around in the mud and snow with lengths of chicken wire that keep getting caught on every twig and, when finally released, immediately roll themselves into their accustomed shape. If the ground isn't frozen, mud splashes up when the digging bar is slammed down to make holes for the posts. Every time you pull out your handkerchief, which is every few minutes, string and wire come out of your pocket and fall in the mud. Other pockets hold tin snips, wire cutters, pruning shears, and a can of Treekote. One pocket has to remain empty for your gloves, which you can't wear while tying the chicken fence to the posts. You put posts all the way around the tree and then, together, wrap the wire fencing around the posts. It never goes all the way around, so you have to get another length with which to piece out. Whatever you find is too long or too short. Your boots stick in the mud, your fingers are cold, your nose runs, a strong cold wind begins to blow, and tempers become short. "Why don't we do this job earlier in the season?" we ask each other.

Molly the dog chases the deer away during the day—and how beautiful they look as they leap across the field and over the hedgerow, white tails flashing! But they seem to know she's inside at night and sneak back into the garden to browse on fruit trees and shrubs. We have seen herds of sixty to seventy deer in the field right beside the garden. The deer are multiplying so rapidly not just because of a lack of predators. The farmers say the deer knock down the corn, which results in the corn picker's missing it. The deer are thus provided with so much food that they multiply and knock down more corn. We used to grieve during hunting season, but no more.

Whatever we can't surround with barriers I spray with rabbit and deer repellent. This evil-tasting stuff is effective except that if forty deer have to find out that they don't like the flavor of your treated blueberry bushes, a certain amount of chewing must take place before they arrive at the decision. I also sprinkle Animal Chaser liberally around and into the evergreen plants that rabbits particularly like, such as armeria, dianthus, *Phlox amoena,* and the azaleas. I let the creatures eat all the *Euonymus fortunei* 'Vegeta' and cotoneaster they want, since I have more than I want. The hope is that if they stuff themselves with it (and they do), they'll let my more precious plants alone (they don't always). Animal Chaser is pretty good, actually, if you remember to strew it often, especially after a new snow. I use it in the summer as well.

Winterizing ceases when it's time to get ready for Christmas and resumes shortly after, when I start collecting used Christmas trees. Every time I go to town, I drive up and down the streets, gathering trees that people have put out by the curb for the trash collector. I stuff them inside the station wagon, as many as will fit, and tie five or six on top. It's not a job I enjoy. I feel the curious eye of the householder upon me, peering out from behind the nylon curtains. Sometimes George, too, will suffer their stares—do they think us so cheap we must pick up their used tree rather than buy a tree before Christmas?—and will collect more on his way home, which I consider above and beyond the line of duty.

You may be wondering why we collect Christmas trees at such great personal sacrifice. You may not know that they provide excellent protection for tender garden plants. They don't pack down, as leaves and straw do. They protect from the winds, trap snow for additional cover, and in theory, at least, reduce the incidence of heaving and thawing by acting as insulation and keeping the ground frozen during unseasonably warm periods.

So I drag my collection of trees toward the border and cut them up with lopping and pruning shears or with the machete that one of my daughters brought back from South America. The branches are laid gently over santolina, flax, chrysanthemums, lavender, heather, silver mound artemisia, anemones, and any other sensitive subject. That's the fun part. I even pile branches around the legs of the least hardy roses.

George complains that in the process I trim the garden with "icicles," those shiny metallic strips that glitter all winter in the sun. I wish people wouldn't put tinsel on their trees, but I can't very well take it all off.

There are, alas, two more serious hazards connected with covering plants for the winter. Families of rodents may move in under the pine boughs, eager to be protected themselves against the cold. There they happily tunnel, build their nests, raise their children, and generally disport themselves to the disadvantage of their hosts. The trouble is, with all those baskets and branches in the way, you can't see what's going on. All winter you gaze at the snow-covered mounds with satisfaction, congratulating yourself on your providence and industry. It's indeed a rude shock to find, in March or April, that while you were defending your plants from one enemy, you were extending an invitation to another. You can put poison in jars laid so that they tilt down, toward the mouth, thus shedding rather than accumulating water and snow. You'll have to check on the jars and replace the bait every month or so if you have as many rodents as I have. Or you can wait even longer to cover your plants, until the rodents will in theory have already chosen their winter quarters. There's always a chance, though, of procrastinating, indecisive, or shiftless rodents happening along, those who failed to make an early selection of cold-weather housing, having thought that Indian summer would last forever.

The second hazard is that in the case of small perennials, the covering prevents you from noticing that they have been heaved loose from their moorings by changes of temperature: Their roots may be exposed and you may not know it. You will have read that mulches and winter coverings put down after the ground is frozen will keep the ground frozen, so that the plants won't be heaved up and out during a break in the weather. It's a comforting but unreliable notion. So, when you go about the garden during thaws in early spring, lift the coverings, and if you find displaced plants, press them back into the ground. If you can't press them back because they are sitting up on a ball of frozen earth, get some nonfrozen earth, which you will have prudently stored in the basement, and cover their roots. If you use cloches, jars, or meter covers on the smaller plants, you can more easily find and check on them.

So much for preparing for winter. We have seen to it that all our plants are properly sited, that they have the soil they prefer, that no plant will dry out or find water settling around its crown and roots. We've covered everything tender with material that neither mats nor stops the air circulation. We've set out rodent bait and wrapped our young shrubs and trees with tape or hardware cloth to foil the browsers. We've sprayed with animal repellent and spread Animal Chaser. We have given all the evergreens a good soaking. We can now relax for a few weeks—at least until it's time to check the wire defenses and the bait jars and renew the repellent spray and powder. How can people go to Florida for the winter?

17

STERLING SILVER

As BEGINNING GARDENERS, we think mostly of flowers, but as we acquire more experience, as we find out how much skill is required to keep a garden looking good all season long, and as we finally realize that most perennials and shrubs carry blossoms for only a few weeks out of the fifty-two, we begin to look for plants whose attractive foliage and growth habits will contribute to the garden scene with or without flowers. We look more carefully at our plants after they've finished flowering and learn to value the individuals who make an effort to keep up appearances instead of letting everything go. We give plants in the first category a more important site and try to tuck the ones in the second behind their more conscientious neighbors. We look deliberately for plants with good foliage – dwarf box, for example, and Japanese ilex, peonies, Siberian iris, the grasses, plants with interestingly colored foliage, whether red, pink, yellow, variegated, or gray.

We become especially fond of gray-foliaged plants. They make quiet, cool areas among the masses of bright colors and peace between flowers whose colors would otherwise fight. More, they often give value to colors that wouldn't have much impact without them. A mauve, lavender, or pale blue flower that would be insipid alone or backed up by green leaves is suddenly elegant against a gray background. Gray mitigates the ardor of unbridled magenta hues. *Geranium sanguineum* can look cheap with certain greens but absolutely smashing surrounded by *Artemisia ludoviciana*. I like to try for a Whistler effect by using grays, whites, and pale pinks, or by placing the grays behind dark red.

The grays are also easy to cultivate. Since most silver-foliaged, gray, or glaucous plants are found growing in high, dry, rocky places in full sun, the smaller ones are eminently suitable for rock gardens, retaining walls, and raised beds. Most of them, small and large, have the simple requirements of sun, poor limy soil, and good drainage. They seem to be disease free and, with the exception of anaphalis and antennaria, almost entirely insectproof. (There is a particularly revolting black caterpillar that attacks those two genera, forcing one either to spray or to be constantly vigilant.) Many of the gray plants can be raised from seed or divided, only a few requiring the use of cuttings for propagation.

The coloring of gray plants is due to a covering of fine hairs that are designed to conserve moisture. A few grays use a combination of scales and hairs; sedums and other glaucous plants have a waxy leaf coating that combined with less noticeable hairs serves the same purpose.

Although some of the most desirable gray-leaved plants, such as *Artemisia arborescens, Senecio leucostachys,* and the helichrysums, cannot be grown outdoors by northern gardeners, be not disheartened. There are masses of hardy grays left to play with—in fact, I've come up with about eighty-five individuals (from thirty-six genera) that can be used in both the perennial border and rock gardens (or their substitutes, like raised beds). Very few of them are difficult to deal with. I am not including the high alpines, however delightful, since their needs are so specialized. The list begins on page 163.

Of the plants listed for the border, two of the tallest and best are *Artemisia ludoviciana* var. *albula* and *A. ludoviciana* var. *ludoviciana.*

Dwarf *Salvia officinalis*

*. . . gray-foliaged plants . . .
make quiet, cool areas among
the masses of bright colors
and peace between flowers
whose colors would otherwise
fight.*

They do pose two problems, neither of which has to do with vulnerability to afflictions. The first is identification. Either or both may be sold as 'Silver King' or 'Silver Queen'. They are almost identical in appearance, especially before their so-called flowers – small white balls in large panicles – are mature. Both are around three feet tall and both have long slender entire or lobed leaves, the only difference being that the leaves of *A.l. albula* (the real 'Silver King') are a bit wider and have more pronounced lobes or teeth. The best way of telling them apart is by their growth habit when flowering. The panicles on 'Silver King' are held straight up; when hung to dry, they make stiff, elongated conical shapes. If you want them to curve gracefully, you must dry them coiled inside a bushel basket. The inflorescences of *Artemisia l. ludoviciana* curl over by themselves in the garden and, when hung, dry in graceful shapes all ready for wreath making. Nurserymen may call this one 'Silver Queen' if they wish, but it should not be called 'Silver King'.

The second problem with these two lovely silvery plants is their determination to take over the whole border. Many gardeners won't plant them in choice places for that reason and confine them to the outer reaches of the property if they grow them at all. It is true that they cause a lot of work, since they have the sneaky habit of traveling underground and coming up in the middle of all neighbors within a radius of four feet. It's pretty exasperating, in the spring, to see those silver shoots eagerly poking their heads up all through the delphiniums, pyrethrums, and especially the iris, which you can't disturb without losing a whole season's bloom. When you get a fork and start lifting the artemisia roots and stolons, you find, running out from the original plants, masses of tangled cords looking like the wires on the outside of a Turkish telegraph office. I'm so fond of these plants that I think the struggle is worthwhile, but I have decided that the best solution is to plant the things in old buckets or cans with the bottoms knocked out. That slows them down a bit. You do have to dig up the whole contraption every other year, divide, and replant.

If you can find it, a better tall and very filigreed frosty artemisia is

A. absinthium 'Lambrook Silver'. It's utterly glorious before it blooms (once finished, though, the faded blooms give it a tarnished look, and it should then be trimmed back), but it isn't the toughest plant in the world. It won't put up with soggy wet clay for very long and in zone 5 it must be thickly covered with pine boughs in winter. 'Lambrook Silver' does not spread—if only it would, just a little. It must be propagated from cuttings taken in spring. That, at least, is the way I have done it. Mrs. Desmond Underwood, an Englishwoman who has written *the* book on silver plants, says cuttings should be taken in July, but then, of course, the newly rooted plants would have to be kept under cover all winter except in areas with mild climates.

A third fine tall gray perennial is Russian sage, usually sold as *Perovskia atriplicifolia,* although it is probably *P. artemesioides.* Never mind—it is a great joy under either name. Its white stems and small, pungent, felty, pinnate leaves are attractive before and after the small, labiate, lavender flowers appear on long panicles in late July. If perovskia is pleased with its situation, a sunny and dry one by preference, it will form a shrub three or four feet high and just as wide—a lovely fountain of silver and lavender. It should be protected in winter and cut back severely in spring.

Achillea 'Moonshine' has flower stems that grow tall—two and a half to three feet—but the tuft of handsome ferny silver foliage remains at a little over one foot. The flat flower heads are of a good bright lemon yellow that does a fine job of harmonizing with the colors of other perennials, even the pinks, and they are produced for many weeks if the old ones are removed regularly. *Achillea taygetea* is a shorter border yarrow, somewhat less gray but with flowers of an even paler yellow over an even longer period. It is the yarrow I use the most in the border. That is, I think what I have is *taygetea.* Some experts who have seen it believe it to be *A.* 'Schwefelblüte', which is very similar.

Everyone knows the globe thistle: The ones usually offered are *Echinops ritro* or *E. humilis* 'Taplow Blue'. The prickly, pinnately dissected leaves of this plant are grayish on top and woolly gray underneath, except in the species *E. spaerocephalis*, which has leaves that are gray on top as well. (The globes on this one are gray white.) When *ritro* and 'Taplow Blue' are in flower, the whole effect is of a mass of blue gray, cool and most effective with the pale yellow *Hemerocallis* 'Hyperion' and the light pink mallow *Malva fastigiata*. There is another echinops available, *E.* 'Veitch's Blue', which has inflorescences of a much deeper blue. It is smaller and shorter than the other globe thistles. *E. bannaticus* is the same deep velvety blue.

Salvia argentea may be a perennial in its native Mediterranean habitat but is a biennial here. The stems that bear white dragon's-head flowers grow to three feet, but the foliage stays near the ground in a large felty rosette two feet in diameter. It is stunning, most unusual foliage – some people grow the plant exclusively for it and cut off the flower stems.

Anaphalis margaritacea is our wild pearly everlasting, which is too accustomed to holding its own against all comers in the fields to be a well-behaved border plant. *A. yedoensis* is somewhat less aggressive but still needs a lot of curbing. I much prefer the six-inch *A. triplinervis*, whose mounds of felty three-ribbed (three-nerved) leaves are extremely handsome all summer. From August through October it gives you the added bonus of corymbs of white everlasting flowers on twelve- to fifteen-inch stems. This plant slowly enlarges its mound but does not send stolons slinking around underground the way the other anaphalis species do. Unlike most grays, *A. triplinervis* likes a bit of shade and doesn't like being parched.

There are tall sedums, eighteen to twenty-four inches, that provide clumps of succulent gray-green-blue foliage all summer, then come out with pink, deep rose, or white flowers in late summer and early fall. *Sedum spectabile* comes in shades of pale, undistinguished pink, as a rule, but *S.s.* 'Meteor' is of a more decisive carmine red, and *S.s.* 'Star Dust', with blue-gray foliage, bears ivory flowers. The best of all for most purposes is *S.* 'Autumn Joy', which is thought to be a cross between *S. spectabile* and *S. telephium*. The blossoms start out a rich pink, then slowly turn to what has been described as salmon-bronze before turning later to coppery red. When they are dark tobacco brown in November, they're good for winter bouquets. 'Autumn Joy' should be divided every few years. I had a large clump that flopped open last year, having gotten too big to maintain its compact shape. I had thought that this subject really was trouble free. I must say it comes as close to being so as any plant I know.

The stems and foliage of the three-foot sea holly, *Eryngium planum,* are not gray but bright blue when the thistly blue flowers open. The stems actually have a metallic sheen. It looks very beautiful planted with the 'Veitch's Blue' echinops. There are many species of handsome eryngiums, but they are difficult to come by in this country. I have failed signally in trying to raise them from seed, losing my patience by the time the second year rolls around, when the seed is supposed to germinate. When I order more exotic-sounding ones, like *E. amethystinum,* or *E. alpinum,* or *E. bourgatii,* they always turn out to look like—to *be,* undoubtedly—*E. planum.* I did raise *E. agavifolium* once, and a splendid, almost terrifying object it was, with great, sharply toothed, swordlike leaves, but of course, it wanted to be back in Argentina where it belonged and died the second winter. *Eryngium planum* never dies and even seeds itself around. It has an extremely long fleshy root, so if you must move it, do it while it's young.

The rest of the grays in the list of border plants are small or medium sized and would be suitable for the front of the border or a few feet back.

My pets are certainly two helianthemums, *H. apenninum* roseum (*rhodanthum* 'Carneum') and *H. nummularium* 'Fire Dragon'. The small opposite leaves on these two plants, narrow and silver, are as handsome as any foliage I know of, and when the single, translucent pink and apricot blossoms appear above the low mounds of foliage, it seems almost too delicious to be true. Cut them back quite sharply when they have finished flowering to keep them from becoming scraggly. These dwarf shrubs would like to be on a wall, but they'll perform faithfully in the border as long as they have good drainage. I lost two of them last summer in my clay flower bed when we had nothing but rain for many weeks. The individuals in raised beds suffered not at all. Helianthemums are of the family of Cistaceae and are called sun roses or rock roses. Although they are a little tender, they will make it through fierce winters even in zone 5 when covered with Christmas tree branches. When you take off the branches in spring, trim the plants back again.

The catmints offered by most nurseries are *Nepeta mussinii* or *faassinii*, but a much better one is *N.* 'Dropmore Variety'. It has smaller, more linear, much grayer leaves and prettier lavender flowers, and it grows taller—to about two and a half feet. It does flop and is best grown through one of those divided metal circles with legs that are made in Scotland but are now sold in America. *Nepeta* 'Dropmore' makes a nice billowy mass of foliage for the long stems of *Geranium wallichianum* 'Buxton's Blue' to wander over and into. The satiny, white-throated blue flowers of the geranium can really be seen and appreciated against the greenish silver background.

Stachys byzantina (lanata), called lamb's ears or savior's flannel, has long been a favorite of children, who love to stroke the woolly gray ears. Gardeners use it where they want either a swath of gray in the flower garden or a ground cover in a hot dry spot. The six- to eight-inch tongue or ear-shaped leaves are so attractive that a nonflowering cultivar is now offered under the name *Stachys* 'Silver Carpet'. Some gardeners like the blooms on the species, which consist of small pale pinky-gray-lavender labiate manifestations (I can't in truth call them flowers) on fourteen- to sixteen-inch racemes. They fail to arouse my enthusiasm, but if you want vertical lines, they provide them for a period of a few weeks, before they get beaten down by the rain. Those who make dried arrangements are very fond of them. I prefer 'Silver Carpet' for situations where height is not needed.

There is another gray plant whose flowers cause a difference of opinion among gardeners. *Santolina chamaecyparissus (incana),* in larger or 'Nana' form, is a neat dwarf shrub that makes a perfect sphere of gray. The foliage, when observed closely, resembles coral. Gray santolina has a wonderful fresh medicinal odor (the green santolina, *S. ericoides* or *virens,* smells of newly pressed olive oil) and produces deep yellow button flowers in July. Some of us shear them off immediately, and others enjoy looking at them. If allowed to flower, the plant tends to lose its spherical form for the rest of the year. All santolinas need winter protection in the North and serious pruning in April.

Of the gray veronicas, *V.* 'Saraband' is unquestionably the best. The foliar color is excellent; it is compact, forming a low mat; and the one-and-a-half- to two-foot flowering dark lilac-blue spikes remain upright – a triumph for any veronica whose besetting sin is to sprawl without even the excuse of having been flattened by a storm. *V. spicata incana* has nice gray foliage, similar to that of 'Saraband', but it never manages to hold more than a third of its flower spikes aloft. The flowers are of a paler lilac blue than those of 'Saraband'. Both of these veronicas bloom from late June to the end of July but will go on for much longer if the spent flowering stems are removed. *V.* 'Minuet' is smaller than the two above, blooms in June, and has spikes of what is described as Tyrian rose. The foliage is very gray in spring but becomes greener as summer progresses. The spikes are almost as inclined to recline as those of *incana.*

You will notice that some of the smaller gray plants are listed for both the rock garden and the border; these are the ones that will accommodate themselves to life on the level in ordinary garden soil. The others on the rock garden list are much better up high in a gritty mixture that includes ground limestone.

The rock yarrows are a delightful group with their furry or toothed leaves, making neat carpets or tufted mounds that look good all year long. Some of them carry small, very white, square-petaled daisies in flattish clusters or corymbs in June; others bear deep or pale yellow yarrow flowers, also on corymbs. One of the prettiest and probably the easiest to grow – certainly the easiest to find – is *Achillea lewisii* 'King Edward', usually listed as *A. tomentosa* 'King Edward'. This is one of the furry ones. The mat creeps close to the ground, and the stems that bear the primrose yellow flowers are about eight to ten inches high. It will bloom almost all summer if deadheaded occasionally. *A. tomentosa* is similar but has flowers of a stronger yellow. Both of these plants absolutely hate prolonged rain and will not hang around long if they're planted in badly drained clay. Get them up high in a good rock-garden mix if you want to keep them. This advice is from one who has lost lots of yarrows in wet clay.

Achillea serbica (sometimes sold as *S. argentea*) has tufts of silvery, fine-toothed leaves and is one of the white daisy sort. A nice little plant—but so are *S. clavennae, A. ageratifolia,* and the others on the list, especially *huteri,* a miniature with almost white foliage.

These gray-white yarrows make a great contribution to the rock garden or to collections of rock garden plants growing in raised beds because they remain compact, are beautiful in themselves, and serve as foils to the bright colors of such plants as dianthus, the penstemons, armerias, silenes, and helianthemums.

Cerastium tomentosum columnae also has very white foliage. It's a big improvement, by the way, on the ordinary snow-in-summer because it is whiter, frostier, lower, and less inclined to infiltrate its neighbors. Five-petaled white flowers on six-inch stems cover the mat in June. *Cerastium biebersteinii* and *C. tomentosum* 'Yo Yo' are said to be better than the old species *C. tomentosum,* but I can't testify from experience because when I sent for them from two nurseries, I received *C. tomentosum.* I should try again.

The twisted, glaucous leaves of *Allium senescens glaucum* are more attractive than its flowers, and *Ruta* 'Blue Beauty' doesn't even *have* flowers, happily, as they would interfere with one's enjoyment of its beautifully designed gray-blue leaves. Its low, tight growth habit is another virtue of this somewhat tender plant.

Anthemis marschalliana (biebersteiniana) is a real doll, as to both foliage and flowers. It grows in a round, flattish, feathery, silver mound, the leaves being deeply divided. Bright, cheerful yellow daisies are held on eight- to ten-inch stems, but the plant would be well worth growing even without them.

All of the shorter artemisias are effective combined with other plants. The best known is *Artemisia schmidtiana,* or silver mound. It seems to be irresistible—thousands of them are sold every year by one grower I know of. Silver mound never exceeds one foot in height, and never spreads. Its one fault is that the hemisphere of soft lacy silver often falls open after flowering (the flowers are almost invisible grayish dots). This unseemly performance will be less likely if you divide the plant in spring after it has shown new growth. In any case, after it has fallen open in July or August, and as soon as new growth can be seen in the center, all the old stems should be removed. This way you stand a chance of having a fresh new silver mound for the latter part of the season.

What is often sold under the name *Artemisia versicolor* may be one of, apparently, two plants: *A. splendens* and *A. canescens.* In *Foliage Plants,* Christopher Lloyd names *A. discolor* as a party to the confusion, but I would forget about that. *Hortus Third* knows nothing about the situation, and the dictionary of the Royal Horticultural Society is no help here, either.

A. versicolor, whether *splendens* or *canescens,* has particularly interesting foliage; like santolina it looks like something that grows under the sea. It, too, stays under one foot but sends up two- to three-foot stalks covered with small, tubular, pale yellow inflorescences. It always looks better in pictures than it does in my garden, perhaps because here it's in the perennial border and is constantly being leaned on by its overenthusiastic bedfellows.

Potentilla villosa is a nice flat creeper with light gray strawberry leaves, producing its yellow flowers in very early spring. Wyman says it is "of little ornamental value." I do not agree with Mr. Wyman, considering it very nice indeed and well worth growing. Other silver potentillas are available for the garden, such as the creeping *P. nevadensis* and the two- to three-foot hairy *P. atrosanguinea.*

Heather, you may know, must not be grown in a limy rock garden and is actually a bit tricky to grow anywhere. It wants a light sandy acid soil with leaf mold and peat moss incorporated therein. No manure and no fertilizer. It likes plenty of rain (or sprinkling), perfect drainage, and a mulch of pine needles. The books always say to plant it in full sun, but American garden books sometimes repeat what the author read in an English garden book. Full sun in England is a different proposition from full sun in most parts of the United States. I find that heath and heather do very well here with morning sun, plenty of light in the afternoon, but no baking. *Calluna vulgaris* 'Silver Queen' is a pretty gray heather, low and spreading, with pale pink-lavender blossoms in late summer. Shear it in spring.

Most dianthus have handsome green-gray or blue-gray foliage, so handsome that they could be grown for foliage alone. Their single and double fragrant flowers are simply a bonus.

Not all the glaucous sedums and sempervivums in circulation are on the list, obviously—just a fair sampling. Once you acquire a taste for these odd things, they're fun to collect and plant in or on a stone wall. They certainly do take care of themselves. My favorite is *Sedum sieboldii*, which sends eight- to ten-inch stems whorling out from one spot in the center. Each stem is set closely its whole length with round, one-inch glaucous leaves that are blue with pink edges, making a wonderful design. This Japanese sedum doesn't bloom until fall, when its pink flowers are most welcome.

As for the ground covers, I will say only that *Lamium* 'Beacon Silver' is a winner, put it where you will. It does prefer a bit of shade. The leaves have a marvelous sheen and the constantly produced flower spikes are of a very good pink.

I include silverweed, *Potentilla anserina*, only to warn you against it. It is so attractive that you might well buy a pot of it at a garden center and spend the next ten years regretting having done so: It moves fast and is utterly irrepressible. Put it only on a rough bank or out by the barn.

GRAY PLANTS

ROCK GARDEN

Achillea ageratifolia
    argentea
    clavennae
    erba-rotta
    huteri
    jaborneggii
    lewisii
    nana
    serbica
    tomentosa
    umbellata
Aethionema grandiflorum
    saxatile
    schistosum
    warleyense ('Warley
    Rose')
Allium senescens glaucum
Androsace primuloides
    (sarmentosa)
    sempervivoides
Antennaria rosea
Anthemis marschalliana
    (biebersteiniana,
    rudolphiana)
Artemisia frigida
    glacialis
    schmidtiana
    'Silver Frost'

versicolor (splendens,
    canescens)
Aurinia saxatilis (Alyssum
    saxatile)
Calluna vulgaris ('Silver
    Queen')
Cerastium tomentosum
    columnae
Dianthus, various
Erigeron compositus
Erodium chrysanthum
Euphorbia myrsinites
Festuca ovina glauca
Hebe decumbens
Helianthemum apenninum
    roseum nummularium
    'Fire Dragon'
Hypericum polyphyllum
    reptans, etc.
Lavandula, various
Orostachys aggregata
    furusei (iwarenge)

Potentilla villosa
Ptilotrichum spinosum
    (Alyssum spinosum
    'Roseum')
Santolina chamaecyparissus
    (incana)
    c. 'Nana'

CONTINUED ON NEXT PAGE

Scabiosa graminifolia
   ochroleuca
Sedum cauticola
   dasyphyllum
   ewersii
   sieboldii
   spathulifolium 'Capa
   Blanca'
Sempervivum arachnoideum
   'Belladonna'
   doellianum
   elegans 'Queen Amelia'
Stachys byzantina
   S.b. 'Silver Carpet'
Thymus vulgaris 'Argenteus'
   lanuginosus
   (pseudolanuginosus)

GROUND COVER

Ajuga 'Burgundy Lace'
   'Silver Beauty'
Cerastium tomentosum
Hosta, certain cultivars
Lamium maculatum
   m. 'Album'
   m. 'Beacon Silver'
   m. 'White Nancy'
Potentilla anserina
Stachys byzantina
   b. 'Silver Carpet'

BORDER

Achillea 'Moonshine'
   'Schwefelblute'
   taygetea
Anaphalis triplinervis
   yedoensis
Anthemis marschalliana
Artemisia absinthium
   'Lambrook
   Silver'
   ludoviciana albula
   l. ludoviciana
   schmidtiana
   'Silver Frost'
   versicolor (splendens,
   canescens)
Aurinia saxatilis (Alyssum
   saxatile)
Dianthus
Echinops
Eryngium
Festuca ovina glauca
Helianthemum apenninum
   roseum nummularium
   'Fire Dragon'
Hosta, certain cultivars
Hypericum polyphyllum
Lavandula
Lychnis coronaria
Nepeta

Perovskia atriplicifolia
Potentilla atrosanguinea
Ruta 'Blue Beauty'
Salvia argentea
Santolina chamaecyparissus
Scabiosa graminifolia
Sedum 'Autumn Joy'
    spectabile

Stachys byzantina
    b. 'Silver Carpet'
Thymus vulgaris 'Argenteus'
Veronica 'Minuet'
    incana
    'Saraband'

18

FACING FACTS

THERE SOMETIMES SEEMS TO BE a conspiracy among people who write about plants to conceal the faults of their subjects. It may be that their fondness for certain plants moves them to write only positively about them, out of loyalty, as it were. As a mother might tell the neighbors that her son is always on the honor roll but fail to mention that he strews his belongings all over the house and runs up fines at the library. We all have our shortcomings, and plants are no exception. I don't think the shortcomings should come as an unhappy surprise to new gardeners. Let the new recruits know of problems that might arise with plants they are considering growing. They will be forewarned and can decide whether they want to take them on. Their experiences might be completely different from ours—they might succeed where we failed—but if they find we were right, at least they won't be resentful. The way to make good, dedicated gardeners is to tell them what they're up against.

And so I regret the consistently high marks that are awarded bearded iris in garden literature. The breeders of these plants have transformed the tough, pretty little peasants that our grandmothers grew into movie queens—gorgeous creatures that are now subject to

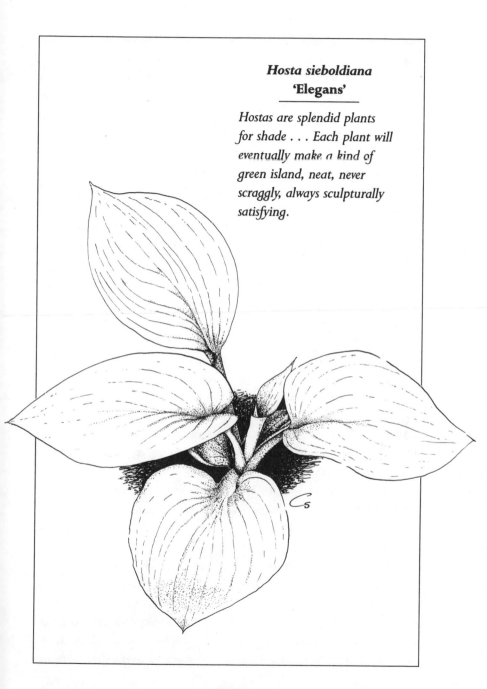

Hosta sieboldiana
'Elegans'

Hostas are splendid plants for shade . . . Each plant will eventually make a kind of green island, neat, never scraggly, always sculpturally satisfying.

borers, root rot, and assorted viruses. They must be deadheaded every day to look neat. They have been made so tall, with blossoms so large, that their stems can no longer support them. Of what use is all that pearly ruffled splendor if it's going to be lying in the mud? I struggled with the things for years, even trying to force stakes down between the rhizomes, dreading the appearance of a storm cloud and breaking my heart when the dazzling beauties keeled over. I finally decided that the emotional, to say nothing of the physical, wear and tear wasn't worth it and sorrowfully dug them up and threw them over the wall. Some of them rooted themselves where they landed and some still come up from pieces of rhizome I missed in the border, but they're strictly on their own now. I enjoy their brief flowers when they produce them, but no more do I clean them up, dust them with sulfur, spray them, stake them, or wail over them. I'm into Siberian and Japanese iris and the small irises now.

Hemerocallis is another genus that's getting a lot of attention from the breeders these days, with a new named variety being born every minute. The coverage of daylilies in the horticultural press is 100 percent positive. They are proposed as the solution for those wanting (and expecting, poor dears) a completely trouble-free, care-free, work-free garden. One gardener has 100 of them in his small city garden and says they never need any attention. Year after year they take care of themselves without spray, fertilizer, or weeding and get better all the time. Another gardener with apparently no more room than the first admits that his 100-plus daylilies are each of a different kind. He's been told he should mass several of each kind together but can't bear to give the space, since he wants them *all*. I have no quarrel with his one-of-each planting system—I am simply showing how much today's articulate gardeners love daylilies.

Now, I have daylilies, too, but I'm not going overboard with them, and I'll tell you why. In the first place their colors rarely harmonize with those of other perennials, so most of them require a place of their own, well away from the flower border if one has a flower border. In the perennial garden I've planted cultivars that were described as "white" or "cream" and had to move them swiftly out again—they were too peachy or orangy yellow to associate with the other border plants. Only the wine-colored purply ones ('Little Grapette', for example) or the pale lemon yellows have worked out. When the breeders finally invent a real white one, though, I'll be the first in line to order it.

The second thing I have against daylilies is that as their gorgeous trumpets fade they hang like wet socks from the tall stalks, looking terribly untidy. If you have time to trot all over the place *every day*, carefully breaking off the dead blossoms (and if you are careless, you'll break off the new buds as well), your eyes will not be afflicted by the sight of limp orange rags dangling from every daylily clump. Even the pale ones turn orange as they shrivel—the red ones turn black—and not all of us have time to remove them. Question: Do those gardeners who have over 100 hemerocallis plants, which may mean thousands of blossoms, deadhead them every day, or are they inured to the wet-laundry look?

Finally, hemerocallis are *not* completely free of disease, despite their reputation. True, whatever makes some of their leaves turn yellow does not prevent them from flowering, but there it is and it's unsightly enough. Under certain conditions they get crown rot and soft rot. The truth is they are comparatively free of disease and fight back bravely when it attacks, but agricultural streptomycin and ter-rachlor are sold as agents for controlling their problems. Which proves they have problems.

Hosta, another hot nursery item these days, also gets a good press. It has always been a toughie, performing under the most trying circumstances. An Old Faithful, marching along cindery driveways, making three-foot strips on the north side of the garage, holding its own in shady sterile yards that otherwise would display only plantain and dandelions. I don't remember its ever showing signs of discouragement or stress. But ha! Now we have dazzling new variegated, crinkle-leaved, blue-leaved, yellow-leaved, and white-leaved hostas, both oriental and Caucasian, sumptuous beauties who are beginning to yellow and wither around the edges in July and August, showing that they are not made of the stern stuff of their plebeian forebears. They, too, are apparently subject to crown rot and possibly botrytis. As for slugs, which spend a lot of their time making lace out of hosta leaves, modern science doesn't seem to have come up with a solution to them. Slug bait must amuse them; it certainly doesn't deter them from going about their appointed tasks. Not that I want to discourage anyone from planting hostas – or hemerocallis either. I just want facts to be faced. Hostas are splendid plants for shade, not because of their flowers, which in most species and cultivars are of little value and are even distracting, but because of the patterns made by their leaves. Each plant will eventually make a kind of green island, neat, never scraggly, always sculpturally satisfying.

So I plead for a straightforward presentation of all the facts about every plant offered as a garden-worthy subject by garden writers, nurserymen, and garden center operators. One shouldn't say that single peonies and dwarf double delphiniums don't need support when they do. One should warn gardeners that tall phlox is prone to mildew and that *Artemisia* 'Silver King' runs all over the border like a maniac. One shouldn't call chrysanthemums "hardy mums" when one knows good and well that they won't survive the winter in zone 5 outside of a cold frame. People should be warned that as the four-foot, much-advertised *Astilbe taquetti* 'Superba' winds up its yearly performance, the spires, starting from the bottom, turn a revolting shade of brown, while the top parts of the flower are still pink.

Beginning gardeners need all the help they can get, and that means being told the truth. If they are deceived, they may become discouraged and not be gardeners any more.

19

THE VOLUNTEER

LAST SUMMER SOMETHING stayed my hand as I was vigorously weeding the west border. A plant with a round, deeply lobed leaf was coming up behind a santolina, its leaves forming a beautiful low rosette. It looked like something. In a few weeks it had sent out running stems that had draped themselves over the santolina and were producing satin cups of a most astonishing hue—red, yes, but not an ordinary cadmium red. Purple red? Crimson? Wine red? It's so hard to describe colors. These glistening red cups were white at the base, and their stamens were united in a tubular column, and the plant was procumbent . . . a poppy mallow, *Callirhoe involucrata,* according to *Hortus Third.*

"How clever of it," I thought, "to choose a gray santolina to lean on!" What if it had been a green santolina—would I have thought it so beautiful? The wine red looked marvelous against the gray, so last fall I moved it to the very front of the west border, where it could romp through a big hummock of the silvery *Anaphalis triplinervis,* which never grows higher than eight inches. Nearby were another gray santolina and the blue-gray foliage of cheddar pinks. Moving along

Callirhoe involucrata

*A plant with . . . round,
deeply lobed . . . leaves forming a beautiful low rosette.*

among these neighbors, the long stems of the callirhoe have been displaying blossoms since May. It is now September 23, the white, fluffy blossoms of the anaphalis have enhanced the picture, and the callirhoe shows no inclination to wind up activities for the season. It has only one flaw — it won't unfurl its petals completely unless the sun is shining on it.

Since it doesn't root as it runs and seems not to impinge on the plants nearby, I am glad to have discovered it. Actually, it discovered me.

20

MORE FACTS

THINK ABOUT ALL THE MANY misrepresentations of plants, the exaggerated praises of catalogs, the misleading photographs, and all your old beginning-gardener's feelings of outrage will come swarming to the surface.

I remember, with pangs of pity for my former guilelessness, poring avidly over the American catalogs I had sent for while planning my garden in Algeria, glorying in the colors, especially the blues. The brilliant cobalt and cerulean blues of the photographs of campanulas and geraniums were fortified by the descriptions. *Geranium grandiflorum* had "vivid . . . ultramarine flowers," G. 'Johnson's Blue' "brilliant bowl-shaped blue blooms." The tall, late veronicas were shown as ultramarine. Catananche was supposed to be a glorious blue, which could be preserved, they said, even in dried arrangements. (When I tried it, the lavender petals dropped off.) Scabiosa, stokesia, platycodon, tradescantia, *Lobelia siphilitica,* and nepeta were all called "blue." I had a mental orgy of blue, from which I didn't recover until several years later, when those campanulas, geraniums, veronicas, and all the others were growing in my garden. My eyes were opened at last and I realized I'd been hoodwinked. I learned in time that there are very few real blue perennials – and that those weren't among them. I've come to like lavender, violet, mauve, and purple, but it's been an acquired taste.

Reds and pinks are also frequently hyped by vendors of seeds and plants. Magenta is usually referred to as crimson or scarlet. (Magenta and purple are both dirty words, apparently.) The whirly-leaved *Allium senescens glaucum* is shown bearing globes of bright pink instead of their washy mauve. *Geranium* 'Birch Double' is pink in the picture but pinky lavender in reality. *G. endressii* 'Wargrave Pink', which has a lot of blue in it, is presented as the clear salmon pink that is found only in *G.e.* 'A.T. Johnson'. *Echinacea purpurea* 'Bright Star', than which no flower is more purply pink, is true pink in most pictures. I have never seen a really pink digitalis except in plant catalogs.

People keep coming to my nursery, catalogs in hand, wanting me to sell them plants that will look like those in the photographs they've been drooling over. I, sadly, have to bring them down to earth – and not only in the area of color.

Sometimes I am, spade poised, about to dig a perennial for a customer (and sometimes I have already dug it) when she'll remark, "Now this will bloom all summer, I understand." The spading stops. I explain that contrary to the claims of advertisers, most perennials bloom for several weeks only, *not* "from June to November" or "May to October," especially where the summers are very hot. Perennials take turns blooming; if you want constant all-summer bloom from one plant, you must buy petunias, marigolds, or some other nonstop annual. The relatively short blooming period of perennials is what makes the garden interesting, I say: it's always changing, and one group of plants takes over as another group finishes. I don't always succeed in persuading the novice; the spade is sometimes returned to the garage while she trails off to buy annuals, obviously feeling I've cheated her, robbed her of her dream of the never-dying, constantly blooming plant. I wouldn't have to spend so much time setting people straight if they hadn't been misled by unscrupulous advertising in the first place. Why does one catalog say, for instance, that *Cimicifuga*

Oenothera missouriensis

*The relatively short blooming
period of perennials is
what makes the garden
interesting . . .*

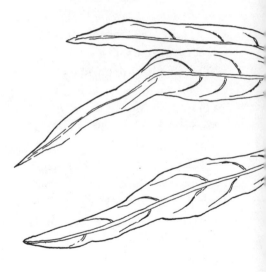

simplex blooms from "early September through late October" when, in the north at least, it starts in October and often is frozen in the bud?

Then there's the question of aggressive plants. I've mentioned *Artemisia* 'Silver King', which is sold as a border perennial by more than one prestigious establishment. And what about lily of the valley? Who warns people about lily of the valley? Like the artemisia, it sends its troops forward underground—under rocks, pathways, and other plants. I'm pretty sure it wouldn't be stopped by a cement sidewalk, so if you want to grow anything other than lily of the valley in your shade garden, you should never let it get started, no matter how much you love its scent. Put it way off under an old lilac bush instead, or along the privet hedge by the driveway. As I fork up bushels of the tangled roots and stolons from my shade garden, I always think, "And they charge money for this!" They even tell you to feed it.

Another lovely stoloniferous menace, *Oenothera speciosa* 'Rosea', is being sold for $6 a plant. After spending his $6, the unwary buyer will have to spend $30 for Roundup to get rid of it. If warned, he could confine it to a rough, sunny bank instead of putting it in his flower garden. Star of Bethlehem *(Ornithagalum umbellatum)* is sold for money, too, whereas it should be outlawed or confined to the wild woods, where it can seed itself to its heart's content and do no harm. I've been pulling and digging it out of my perennial garden for seventeen years.

One nursery admits that *Lysimachia clethroides* is a land pirate but describes *L. punctata* (yellow loosestrife) as an ideal plant for the border. Instructions are given for its care. Actually, the lout would thrive and spread in the middle of a football field during playing season.

Some stoloniferous shrubs are also sold as companions to perennials. They shouldn't be. I believed an advertisement and purchased that very pretty red-stemmed, variegated dogwood *Cornus alba* 'Elegantissima'; the surrounding primulas, astilbes, and trollius have since had to fight desperately for survival against the dogwood's insatiable surface roots and ever-advancing stolons. I can't even dig out the wild garlic that's got in around it, as the trowel can't penetrate the tangle.

Two undisciplined yarrows that are presented as border plants have, in my opinion, no business at all in a border and belong instead in a cutting garden—*Achillea millefolium rosea* and *A. ptarmica* and their cultivars. Some nurseries do warn about the latter, and also about the spreading propensities of sweet woodruff. I wish I'd been warned.

But how many nurseries caution us about the self-seeders? Feverfew, brunnera, *Malva fastigiata,* and *Campanula rotundifolia* are probably the worst, and one should be told to fly at them with pruning shears and cut off their dead blossoms before they make and scatter seed. At least hoeing and troweling up seedlings is not as exasperating a job as trying to extricate invading stolons from the roots of neighboring plants.

It's a great help now to have the hardiness zone numbers given for each plant listed in a catalog—as long as they're reasonably accurate. But I've found the tender tricolor sage listed for zones 3–9 and *Ruta* 'Blue Beauty' for zones 4–9. My rues usually winter under bushel baskets and still look pretty peaked in the spring. Geums, which rarely make it through our winters even under pine boughs, have been said to be zones 5–9. *Aethionema* 'Warley Rose', that fragile little princess that shivers and sulks even under a cloche and evergreen branches, I've found listed for zones 4–8. I'm lucky if I bring it through two or three winters here. Blue flax is just barely and possibly accidentally perennial, I've decided, and yellow flax frankly gives up when the going gets rough in December, yet both are sold as hardy perennials.

My greatest disappointment—and financial loss—has been from buying, loving, and losing dianthus, "hardy" carnations and perpetual pinks, mostly those delicious double dianthus with such names as 'Helen', 'Ian', 'Doris', and 'Blanche'. I have had to conclude they are not for me, no matter who says they'll survive zone 5, and must content myself with dianthus species, mat formers, and *D. plumaris* in various forms.

While I'm fulminating I may as well declare that biennials, such as

Eryngium giganteum and Canterbury bells, shouldn't be sold as perennials. Nor should chieranthus (wallflower) and other plants that behave in cold climates like biennials, such as *Salvia argentea, S. haematodes,* and *Digitalis mertonensis,* be peddled to the innocent as hardy. And shouldn't the innocent always be told that real French tarragon can't be propagated from seed and the tarragon that can is useless? Or that plain *Origanum vulgare* makes good dried flowers but is not very good for cooking? (The Greek oregano, *O.v. hirtum,* also listed as *viride* or *heracleoticum,* is the real thing. See Gertrude Foster's *Herbs for Every Garden.*) Should those herbaceous potentillas that send out great wandering stems in all directions be pictured as compact masses of color? Should lavender be sold as hedge material anywhere but in the South, when in the North it looks wretched for many weeks in the spring? Should seed companies make false promises about perennials that cost the unfortunate plant grower two years of wasted effort? Should nurseries neglect to alert buyers that a plant is disease prone or liable to attack by certain insects, that it must have serious staking, that its habit is to drop its petals or close its flowers at noon?

It would be better not to make the customers find these things out for themselves. But in this imperfect world it is no doubt too much to expect that the vendor will volunteer such information; if he answers questions truthfully, it's probably good enough. After all, gardeners should certainly do their homework, read books, and experiment on their own. They needn't be spoon-fed. So if a catalog consists of a simple list of plants, their heights, colors, soil requirements, blooming periods, and no other information, one cannot find too much fault with it. Silence is not the same as misrepresentation. But when the buyer is convinced that a flower is a color it isn't, that a ruthless spreader is a good garden plant, that a plant is trouble free when it's often victimized by botrytis blight (lilies), rust (hollyhocks), root rot (lupines), or mysterious viruses (gypsophila), he has been dealt with dishonestly. And dishonesty is always, in the end, destructive.

21

YARROWS

CERTAIN GENERA SEEM TO HAVE contributed more than their share of good garden plants. What would we do without all the different campanulas, for example: tall, medium, and short ones for the flower border, and miniatures for rock walls and raised beds? Iris come in all colors and sizes, from three or four inches to six feet tall, and for every kind of site, from swamps to sandy dry spots. Certainly yarrows, too, are indispensable in their variety of species and cultivars. Not only do they come in different sizes, they also contribute much in the way of interesting foliage; most are hardy; they are neither attractive to insects nor prone to diseases; and the pungency of their foliage adds much to the joy of working with them.

Most yarrows have the great virtue of not needing staking. The ones that fail to hold themselves upright don't make very good candidates for the perennial border for more reasons than their tendency to recline. Almost all yarrows want full sun, a spare soil, and good drainage. Their ability to withstand drought is another point in their favor. They can all be divided easily, either in spring or early fall, and the species come fairly readily from seed. With a few exceptions they endure extremes of cold and heat with perfect equanimity.

Achillea 'Moonshine'

. . . lemon-yellow heads that blend better with many border plants than do those of deeper gold . . . Try it planted near a group of Salvia superba *'Blue Queen' or 'East Friesland'.*

Aside from the wild white yarrow *(Achillea millefolium)*, the yarrow most people are familiar with is the tall yellow one, *A. filipendulina (eupatorium)*, in either the species or the special forms, such as 'Parker's Variety' or 'Gold (Golden) Plate'. This one is a stout, three- to four-foot, many-stemmed plant whose pinnate green leaves, up to ten inches long, give it a ferny appearance. The flowers are large flat heads of deep yellow, sometimes five or six inches across, that are handsome in the garden and good dried in winter bouquets. 'Gold Plate' produces the largest heads.

An even more stately plant is *A.* 'Coronation Gold' *(A. filipendulina × A. clypeolata)*. Because one of its parents has lacy gray leaves, the foliage of 'Coronation Gold' is handsomer and more silvery than that of its other parent. It grows to about three feet, carries heads of the same deep gold as *A. filipendulina,* and is just as good for drying.

Alan Bloom crossed *A. clypeolata* with *A. taygetea* and created one of the best of all yarrows, 'Moonshine'. It has a large tuft of very silvery, fluffy, deeply lobed foliage at its base. The flower stems rise from this low tuft to two and a half feet and carry lemon-yellow heads that blend better with many border plants than do those of deeper gold. Once it starts blooming in June, it will go on for most of the summer if it is deadheaded. Try it planted near a group of *Salvia superba* 'Blue Queen' or 'East Friesland'.

While appreciating the virtues of 'Moonshine', I would still nominate *A. taygetea* as the best yellow to use in a border of perennials whose colors run mostly to pinks, lavenders, and blues. The foliage of *A. taygetea* is grayish but not as gray or as stunning as that of 'Moonshine'. It has three advantages, however, over its competitor: it remains quite short, generally around one and a half to two feet; it starts blooming in May and goes on until a hard frost if the blossoms are removed as they turn dingy; the flowers are sulfur yellow, the palest of all, so they go with everything. Naturally, if you have a garden of hot colors—vermilion, orange, flame red—you will want 'Coronation Gold' instead.

The *Achillea clypeolata* that helped produce 'Coronation Gold' and

'Moonshine' is one that doesn't seem to be sold in this country. Graham Stuart Thomas is very fond of it and describes it so enticingly that one feels frustrated at not finding it listed anywhere, either as plants or seeds. He says the leaves on this twenty-inch plant are "the most silvery imaginable . . . like palest jade-green feathers." Alan Bloom says it sends up a long succession of deep yellow heads, flat and dense. Both writers admit it's inclined to die out if it isn't divided frequently or if the drainage isn't perfect.

There are two other tall yarrows that are frequently used in flower borders but that I usually relegate to the cutting garden because of their relentless colonizing instincts. The first is *A. millefolium*. The garden forms of this species are usually cerise red or rosy pink. They have extremely ferny green leaves and the unforgivable habit of diving underground and resurfacing just where you want them the least.

Another fault is their floppy stems. One does get cross with flowers that don't make it their business to stand up straight. These failings, in the case of *A. millefolium* 'Red Beauty', 'Fire King', or 'Rosea', are all the more annoying because the flowers are charming, being two-toned with an appealing, old-fashioned look, like that of printed calico. I have a couple of the pink forms back in a rough part of the border; they stand up better than the red ones, but I have to fall on them severely with mattock and spade every year or so to keep them in line.

The other vandal is *A. ptarmica,* even the lovely form called 'Angel's Breath', which is an improvement on 'The Pearl'. They are both double, very white button flowers, wonderful in bouquets. Dried they are cream colored rather than white but still attractive. In addition to being aggressive, *A. ptarmica* has less than outstanding foliage and growth habits. The leaves are linear, not pinnate or lobed—they don't look at all like the leaves of the other tall yarrows. They're about two to three inches long, come straight out of the lanky lax stems, and are inclined to mildew in hot humid weather, although the species choose damp sites in the wild. If you like to keep flowers in the house, grow this one despite its shortcomings. It's worth some trouble for its value as a cut flower.

Graham Thomas lists another three-foot border yarrow, *A. grandifolia*, from Asia Minor. After describing its "tiny white daisy flowers, held in good flat heads," its deeply lobed lacy gray foliage, and its long blooming period, he then remarks that it's a "rare and neglected plant." If he thinks it's neglected in England, he should see what use is being made of it in America. Since it doesn't appear in any catalog or on any seed list in general circulation and isn't even listed in *Hortus Third*, I hope he realizes that we gardeners are not to be held responsible for neglecting it. It's just another name to put on our want lists, hoping we can eventually track it down—without having to go to Asia Minor.

The yarrows furnish us with many excellent rock garden plants, some of them having silver-gray foliage and corymbs of small chalk-white, square-petaled daisies, usually with buff centers. Another group has green or gray mossy foliage, close to the ground. Their flowers may be either white or yellow. Some of these plants are available from specialty nurseries, and others can sometimes be found in the seed exchange lists of alpine plant societies.

One of the more common rock yarrows is *A. tomentosa*, offered either as the species or as the varieties 'Moonlight' and 'Aurea'. The plant has flat furry foliage that is greenish when wet and gray when it's dry. It spreads along rocks or the ground, sending up flowers on twelve-inch stems from June on. It hates continuous rain and swampy conditions and will dwindle away in soggy clay. Up on a gritty height it will flourish. The species and 'Aurea' bear deep yellow flowers, but 'Moonlight' has very pale yellow blossoms on erect stems.

Some catalogs list *Achillea* 'King Edward' as *tomentosa*, but it is actually a cross between *A. tomentosa* and *A. clavennae* and should be listed as *A. lewisii*. It is an enchanting plant with very gray ground-hugging foliage, bearing its pale primrose-yellow flowers all summer long. The flowers fade to cream and never look unsightly.

In a raised bed here I grow a plant that I bought as *A. argentea* but that is probably *A. serbica*. Many of the low silvery yarrows are so similar that there is a certain amount of confusion among the experts as to their identity. *A. argentea,* from Yugoslavia, is described by two authorities as having three-lobed, silver-white leaves and white flowers on five- to six-inch stems. I won't go into *Hortus Third*'s ideas on the subject, which are quite different. My plant is about four inches high, flowers at about six inches, has gray, minutely toothed leaves, un-lobed, that grow in tufts. Awfully nice, whatever it is.

I have two other small silver yarrows that I enjoy tremendously— *A. huteri* and *A. jaborneggii*. *Huteri* is a species from Switzerland, and *jaborneggi* is a cross between *A. clavennae* and *moschata*. They are both tufted, like *serbica*. *Jaborneggii* makes a slightly higher and wider mound than *huteri,* and its toothed leaves are not quite so white. The *huteri* leaves are . . . I am tempted to say adorable; they're like little white hands, deeply lobed. Both plants smother themselves in small white daisies, *huteri* from May to July, *jaborneggii* from June to August. They couldn't be nicer.

I might think *Achillea ageratifolia* v. 'Aizoon' (*Anthemis* 'Aizoon') nicer if I had one; Walter Kolaga, Wyman, and Beth Chatto all give it very high marks. Of course, all I have to do is read "bi-pinnate leaves, silvery-pubescent" to begin to covet. Lincoln Foster, who apparently has never had the gray fever, is not moved to rhapsodize over any of these rock garden yarrows and says only that they can furnish a contrast to and "break up the splashes of their more brilliant neighbors, an important if inglorious role." I've presented his opinion, to be fair, but I don't really want anyone to be influenced by him in this case.

There are several others in this group of yarrows that sound interesting—the Swiss *A. decolorans (serrata), A. nana* from southern Europe, *A. umbellata,* another Greek, *A. clavennae,* which grows in the Alps, and *A. erba-rotta* ssp. *rupestris (A. rupestris)* from the Apennines. I'd like to have the whole lot.

Beth Chatto says *A. decolorans* 'W. B. Child' has finely cut green leaves and prefers to be cool. She says the lacy clusters of white flowers are good for cutting, which could be, since this one grows to eighteen inches. Described as tolerating heavier soil and moister conditions than most members of its family, it blooms from May to August, when it should be cut back sharply. The common name of *A. decolorans* is "mace."

Achillea nana, known as chamomile of the glaciers, has mats of finely cut, downy green leaves one inch high and clusters of white flowers in densely rounded corymbs on six-inch stems most of the summer. This one wants to be hot and dry. *A. erba-rotta* ssp. *rupestris* has rosettes of narrow green lance-shaped scalloped leaves and showy clusters of white flowers six to eight inches above the mat from May to July. It has a strong, pleasant aroma. The long narrow soft leaves of *A. umbellata* make gray-green clumps, and white flowers appear on ten-inch stems in May and June. Easy to grow, they say.

A. clavennae is one of the better-known rock yarrows. It sounds very similar to *ageratifolia, argentea,* and *serbica* — tufted, hoary, four to ten inches. The deeply lobed leaves are white, silky and tomentose; the plant bears loose corymbs of white flowers, which one writer says are more numerous than those of *argentea.*

There is another yarrow that doesn't belong with either the rock or border yarrows but is an herb that has always been held dear by those who love spicy fragrance. *Achillea ageratum,* sweet nancy or sweet maudlin, is a not-very-dramatic individual that has notched green leaves and yellow flowers in its season. It grows to about one and a half feet. Thompson & Morgan sells seeds of this old favorite but wrongly describes it as having a rosette of silver foliage. Wyman says it is for zone 7, but a friend is growing it here in zone 5.

We think of the wild white yarrow as being an American native. Actually, it is native of Britain, southern Europe, and Asia and has been taken from those places and naturalized pretty well all over the temperate regions.

Pliny says *Achillea millefolium* got its name from Achilles, who used it on his soldiers during battle to staunch the flow of blood from their wounds. We know the Greeks and others used it for this purpose; some of its folk names are soldiers' woundwort, sanguinary, and nosebleed. Several species of yarrow *(moschata, millefolium,* and *ageratum)* have been cultivated as medicinal plants in Europe and Asia. In the seventeenth century *A. millefolium* was added to salads and for many years was put into fermenting beer to improve the flavor and make it more potent. It has been used in our time—and may still be—to flavor both soft and alcoholic drinks. Native Americans used *A. lanulosa,* a native American species, as medicine. The Chinese use it medicinally and in the divination ritual of I Ching. The Saxons used yarrow both for protection against evil and as an aid in casting spells, having it both ways. Have you ever heard of a more useful plant?

22

BULBS

A VISITOR TO MY GARDEN once observed my *Gentian septemfidas* growing in the woods garden. "I put mine in lime in the sun and they do beautifully!" he said.

"Good luck to you!" I said to myself testily. "Mine would die in short order if I did the same."

I have seen a friend's *Salvia pitcheri (S. azurea* var. *grandiflora)* unstaked, making an arching but upright shrub of itself, a fountain of glorious blue; in my border the stems sprawl so gracelessly that they detract from the lovely blossoms. If she were to write about *Salvia pitcheri,* she'd say never mind staking it, whereas I would say it must be staked.

The other fellow is not necessarily wrong when he gives garden advice that we don't agree with: His experience may have been different from ours. Certain facts are incontestible – ericaceous plants prefer an acid soil, ligularia wants moisture – but aside from such certainties, so much depends on differences in light, moisture, soil, drainage, climate, and microclimate.

So now I wish to differ with almost all of the horticulture experts whose books I've read. They are keen on bulbs. They discuss the

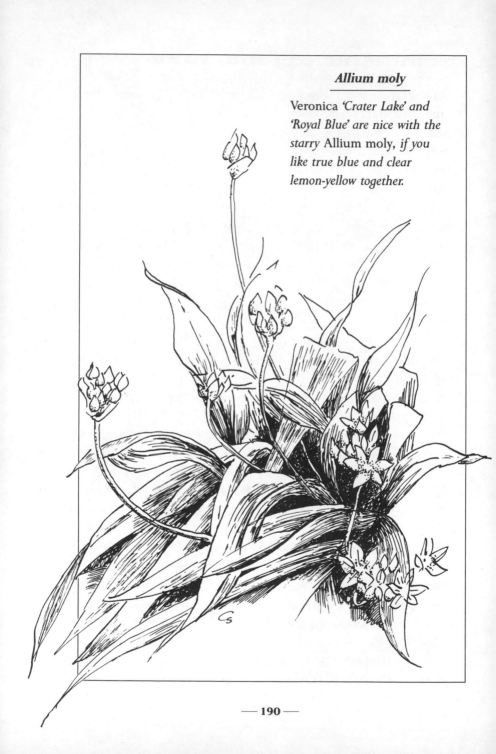

Allium moly

Veronica *'Crater Lake'* and *'Royal Blue'* are nice with the starry Allium moly, *if you like true blue and clear lemon-yellow together.*

subject at length and tell us how they struggle to master their passion but inevitably succumb to the lure of the catalog pictures and order hundreds more bulbs every year. This yielding is a thing I can't understand. Unless they have a woods or unless the chipmunks are eating them all, where are they putting them? How can they find room for everything else it takes to make a garden? How do they cope with them in the perennial border? Because inevitably they put them in the border and take it for granted that we will do the same.

I struggled for five or six years, trying to use tulips and daffodils in the border, and discovered their two weaknesses. In the first place, if you have clumps of them here and there all through the garden, they look pretty silly putting on a show when all their neighbors are either still underground or just beginning to emerge. Almost the only color to keep them company is that of the new red spears of the peonies. In the second place, they don't last very long, due to our usual May heat wave, and sit there, getting yellower and uglier every day. Since one knows that one daren't cut off the tops, which are feeding the bulbs, one is trapped into looking at the mess through June and well into July, if I remember rightly. I *know* one is supposed to have a handy gypsophila or some other exuberant subject nearby whose flowers or foliage will hide the terminating tulips, but somehow I've never been able to pull it off. Either the baby's breath dies in the winter, or the rabbits eat the cover-up candidate I've provided, or I've forgotten to provide one at all. I've thought of lifting up the bulbs and replanting them out by the barn, where they can mature their foliage and look ugly out of harm's way, but that's a lot of work at a time when one is already swamped. I'll bet that's the solution of people with more help than I have. Or they throw out the bulbs, plant annuals in their place, and put in new bulbs in the fall. The photographs of masses of tulips and daffodils being gorgeous in flower borders or in elegant plantings around front doors always madden me. Why don't they print a picture of the same area two weeks later?

Then there's the business of accidentally spearing the bulbs after the wretched things have finally gone dormant. In late summer you see a vacant spot in your border and wonder why it doesn't have a tenant. You plunge your spade down to prepare a hole for planting something and find you have sliced into a whole family of tulips. You try to get over your guilt feelings by blaming the bulbs for lying there so furtively, not saying anything.

I thought, years back, that I had a brilliant plan for daffodils. I had literally bushels of old King Alfred I'd found and saved as I dug up the weeds to make a garden, so I planted them three or four deep just this side of the long low stone wall. Thus, I thought, all the perennials that would be surging up later between the daffodils and a garden viewer would really hide the disintegrating foliage (the depth of the border varies from four feet to thirty-two). It worked out well for several years until grass and wild asters got into the daffodils. I couldn't get rid of the weeds without lifting those hundreds of bulbs and starting over, which seemed too formidable a task. Little by little I'm replacing the daffodils with tall perennials that I can keep clear of weeds more easily.

The place for bulbs, I've decided, is in the woods garden or drifting around shrubs or trees, and I do *not* mean planted in circles around them. In a woodland area where the trees are deciduous the bulbs will have sunlight when they need it, in early spring, and they will all be having their big moment at roughly the same time of year. If you have small bulbs started—snowdrops, chionodoxa, the scillas, anemones, grape hyacinths, species crocuses, and erythroniums—they will begin the show, so that the whole area will be looking festive when the daffodils and tulips appear. By the time the trees leaf out, the bulb plants will be able to dispense with sunlight. They can all peacefully and inoffensively mature their foliage, as by then you will be concentrating your attention on the perennial border, where everything will be ready to carry on. Another reason for putting the bulbs in a wooded area is that very few weeds will go where they can't get summer sun.

If you plant bulbs near trees and shrubs, you should put them in areas that need not be mowed before the bulb foliage dies down, and where you won't mind a shaggy look for a number of weeks. Species crocuses and many of the other small bulbs make a swift and graceful exit compared with that of tulips or daffodils. Under an old white pine on the front lawn I have a mass of *Crocus tomasinianus*—as many as the chipmunks allow me to keep—that spreads itself out like a sultan's jewel collection; the area doesn't produce much grass, and the few blades that do appear don't look too unkempt before they can be cut. I don't cut the grass with scissors, as they did around bulbs planted in the lawn at John Loudon's house near London, but if that's what it took to have those translucent amethyst cups with their orange-scarlet stigmas sprinkled under the pine tree in my garden, I think I'd do it.

23

ASTERS

I WONDER WHY MORE PEOPLE don't go in for perennial asters. Granted, they bloom wild all over the fields in shades of pale lavender and purple. For that reason even I wouldn't plant the tall lavender or purple asters as long as I can enjoy all that color without going to any trouble. Especially here in the country, the fields that surround the garden are so full of wild asters that they make a purple haze all around in late summer and fall—and also move in when I'm not looking. I'm always pulling yards of their stolons out of the clumps of phlox and baptisia, or trying to.

Many of the garden varieties of our native asters, *novae-angliae* and *novi-belgii*, have been developed in Europe, mostly in England, where they are called Michaelmas daisies and are highly thought of. Lots of the cushion-type *novi-belgiis*, however, are the work of breeders in the United States and Canada. They have crossed *Aster novi-belgii* with *A. dumosa* and with *A. subspicatus (douglasii)*, aiming for good color, compact form, and resistance to rust and mildew.

When I started my garden some years ago, I planted some of the tall New England asters, *N.a.* 'Harrington's Pink' and 'September Ruby', but found two things wrong with them besides the fact that

Aster alpellus 'Triumph'

*It is a triumph . . . a mat
former whose blooming stems
never go above twelve inches.*

they close toward evening and need staking. Possibly owing to the way I was handling them, the leaves on the bottom two-thirds of the stems always turned brown before the tops burst into bloom, and they bloomed so late that they were usually ruined by frost just as they were hitting their stride. If they had been given extra water during our usual August dry period, their leaves might not have shriveled—I don't know. At that time I didn't have a deep well, so what water I had was used to save desperate plants from dying outright. Simple stress didn't warrant a plant's being given a drink.

Not being satisfied with the way the tall asters performed here, I decided to try dwarf *novi-belgii* cultivars, since many of them not only stayed low but bloomed earlier than the others. And what a joy they have been! They make tidy, ten- to fifteen-inch mounds of small dark green leaves that really do cover themselves all over, starting in late August or early September, with single or semidouble composite flowers. You can work out a perfect symphony of color with them in the front of your border or perhaps near shrubs or trees in part shade. One summer I planted a swath of them in the front of my border in this order: white, pale lavender, dark violet-blue, pale pink, deep pink, carmine, then the whole thing reversed on the other side, ending again in white. Since I had several of each color and they billowed around a bit, it didn't look too self-conscious or regular and was, I say modestly, absolutely dazzling.

Almost all the mail-order nurseries sell an assortment of these plants, or they can be found potted at garden centers. There are a few tall *novi-belgii* asters on the market, so look carefully and learn the eventual height of the ones you are buying. Of the dwarfs, I like 'Persian Rose', a good pink with yellow in it rather than blue, and 'Alice Haslam', a double deep rose. 'Winston Churchill', eighteen inches and early, is an intense shade of what the nurseries call red but I would call carmine. 'Alert' is similar but borders more on magenta. 'Royal Opal' is pale lavender-blue with a noticeable yellow eye, a beautiful plant. My very favorite is 'Professor Kippenberg'. It's not pure blue but it comes close to it—a clear medium violet-blue that is simply a knockout. There are several whites on the market: 'Snow Cushion' and 'White Fairy', both ten inches, and 'Snow Flurry', eighteen inches. 'Bonningdale' is a taller double white at two and a half feet. There are so-called blues at various heights, from twelve inches to three feet and of shades that vary in intensity. Nurseries say that 'Sailor Boy' is "navy blue," which I translate as dark violet-blue or purple, although I have not yet seen it. I'd like to try more of the taller *novi-belgii* asters, but so far I have not been very pleased with them. 'Blue Gown', described as a three-foot "clear sky blue," looked just like the wild purple field flowers to me, which, as I say, are beautiful but free.

The *novae-angliae* asters are always at least two and a half to three feet tall and sometimes taller, rising as high as four or five feet. The only one I've dealt with in the last few years is a splendid individual called 'Alma Potschke', whose color is an indescribable salmon-rose, a very vibrant hot pink with no blue at all in its composition. Its growth habit is also remarkable: although it will attain two and a half feet, it covers itself all over with flowers instead of blooming only on the top of long brown stems.

Since looking seriously at perennial asters, I've tried several species and found that one can have asters blooming through much of the growing season. With the early true *Aster alpinus* I haven't been notably successful, either with purchased or seed-grown plants. They weren't terribly attractive and they didn't bloom for long. No doubt they prefer alpine conditions to anything I can offer them. The nurseries offer one called *A. alpellus* 'Triumph' that is a cross between *A. alpinus* and the European *A. amellus*. It is a triumph for its breeder. This small aster is a mat former whose blooming stems never go above twelve inches. The one-and-a-half-inch flowers are the usual aster blue with deep yellow centers, but they have good substance and are produced for many weeks, starting in May. The plant never seems to have any problems.

The next one to bloom is the Chinese *Aster tongolensis (yunnanensis)* 'Napsbury', another mat former but on a larger scale. The three-and-a-half-inch leaves on this plant are stalkless and oblong. Its "blue" daisies on twelve- to fifteen-inch stems are enormous wide-awake creations with almost orange centers; the blooming period is May through much of June. Everyone who sees it for the first time wonders why he has never seen it before. I myself can't think why it is not planted more often.

July may be asterless if 'Triumph' has stopped performing, but August and September are covered by the *novi-belgii* cultivars, and in September begin the *novae-angliaes*. 'Alma Potschke' blooms for easily six weeks. There is another *Aster tongolensis*, 'Wartberg Star', that is said to bloom in July and August. It is twenty-four inches tall and lavender-blue.

In areas slightly warmer than mine the eighteen-inch *Aster thomsonii* 'Nanus' will be in flower from July onward. The foliage is gray-green, the flowers lilac-blue. Its only shortcoming is that the petals are not quite wide and dense enough. The books say this aster is for zone 6 and warmer, as are the two *Asters frikartii* 'Wonder of Staffa' and 'Mönch', which were created in Switzerland by crossing *A. thomsonii* with *A. amellus.* Also nonstop bloomers, they are extremely fine plants that grow to around three feet, freely branching and producing masses of elegant lavender daisies. 'Mönch' is rated the better plant of the two, as it has more perfect flowers of a better color and never needs staking. I grieve that the climate is just a bit too cold here for *frikartii*—one winter out of two it can't make it through until May. Perhaps I'll get 'Mönch' and put it in the cold frame in November.

I know of no yellow asters for cold climates; the plant sold as *Aster* 'Golden Sunshine' is really *Chrysopsis mariana*, a three-foot fall-blooming composite that in my garden was less than impressive. It looked like the humble field flower it is in Maryland, with a bunch of small yellow daisies on top of one long bare-looking leg. I'll leave it for another year and see whether it will become bushier. I always believe in giving something a second chance.

I've tried growing a few of the asters from seed (Thompson & Morgan has a long list), among them *A. alpinus* 'Dark Beauty', a purple one, and *A.a.* 'Happy End', a semidouble pink. They did what they were supposed to do—made mats and produced their blossoms—but as I said, they didn't lift my heart. I'd rather give the space they occupied to something more dazzling or at least more interesting. You can get seed for the amellus hybrids and even for *A. frikartii* and some *novae-angliae* cultivars, such as 'September Ruby', but surely they will not consistently reproduce their parents.

Asters will grow in full sun or light shade (the dwarfs seem to benefit from being spared the afternoon sun), in acid or neutral soil. They insist on an adequate amount of moisture and will not thrive in a sterile dry spot. Neither do they want to be waterlogged in winter. Give them reasonably good soil, extra water during dry periods, and nourishment in the form of manure or compost, and see how well they perform.

As for diseases and other problems, asters are reputedly prone to mildew and wilt, but I have had no trouble with either of these. If your plants look as if they are planning to become mildewed, dust them with sulfur or spray them with Funginex, the latter being a longer-lasting preventive. Mildew, of course, doesn't hurt plants but does offend the eye of the beholder. As for wilt, the only remedy is to destroy all sick plants immediately. I *have* had to watch out for insects, lace bugs, I believe, and I admit to spraying the plants several times a season with something that eliminates sucking insects. The warning sign is a sort of gray, speckled, scruffy deposit on the leaves.

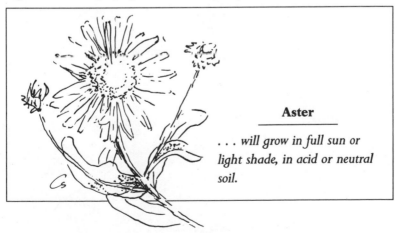

Aster

. . . will grow in full sun or light shade, in acid or neutral soil.

Tall New England asters don't require division more often than every two years, but the dwarf *novi-belgiis* seem to dwindle away or become weak if they are not divided every spring. They send out stolons from the mother plant even as they are blooming in September, so the procedure is to get well under each plant with a spading fork and lift the whole confusing mass out of the ground. Sit down comfortably where you can keep the roots out of the sun and wind, and patiently separate them, wiggling or cutting off good stout little pieces that have healthy roots and putting them immediately into a plastic bag. Discard the center part, which will have the remains of woody stems and probably very little root left. Plant your divisions in good soil about a foot or more apart and shade them with pine boughs or loose straw for almost a week, until the roots begin to function again. Although it's hard to believe when you plant them, each little piece will make a mound of colorful bloom by late summer.

24

ROCK PLANTS

THE IDEA OF GROWING ROCK PLANTS appeals to many people. Often, however, they are daunted at the outset by two widely held notions: that rock plants are extremely difficult to grow and that a rock garden is required to accommodate them. It is certain that true alpines, whose homes are on high mountains above the tree line, are not easily made happy in the lowlands, especially in regions with long, hot, muggy summers. If you happen to have a moraine—a shaley slope with ice water running beneath the shale—you may be able to persuade them that they are on a mountaintop, being watered by melting glaciers. Or if you have an alpine house, where you can give them cool air as well as stone chips and cold water, you may succeed in raising those delightful little saxifragas, soldanellas, and other prima donnas of the heights. But even if such high-alpine plants are not for all of us, there are many good plants that are perfectly cheerful so long as they have gritty soil and sharp drainage.

Building a rock garden is actually unnecessary—happily, since it is so often done with lamentable results. The amateur enthusiast may construct something resembling a large Christmas pudding or a giant chocolate chip cookie in a corner of his yard. It relates to nothing else

Wall garden

As the wall garden becomes established, the plants will seed themselves into other crevices, so that it will really take care of itself.

within sight and has perhaps a dozen unhappy little plants huddled mournfully among a collection of disparate rocks set on the ground or partially embedded therein.

A rock garden can be superlatively beautiful if it is sited to look like an integral part of its surroundings. It should be located well away from buildings. If one is not one of the fortunate few with a rocky hillside or outcroppings, one must make the rocks *look* like a series of outcroppings. To do it well is not easy—indeed, it is a major operation. The smaller the garden, the harder it is to make it look natural. There are those of us who have neither the time nor the money to construct—much less maintain—one of these delights.

There are two possible alternatives. The first is to construct a wall garden. If there is a slope to the site under consideration, one can build fairly easily a dry retaining wall (one without mortar) that will furnish a fine home for saxatile plants. In fact, the wall solves two problems if it is replacing a slope one has been trying to keep mowed—an exasperating task.

When the line of the wall has been determined, whether curved or straight, the earth should be dug down about six inches, any weed roots removed, and gravel put down before the first course of stones is laid. The stones should be as flat as possible, and the more similar they are in appearance, one to another, the better the wall will look. As you build you should put a one- to two-inch layer of prepared soil between the layers and ram it well in behind the rocks, leaving no air pockets. This packing is to give the plant roots solid earth to move back into and also to keep the wall from eventually buckling after prolonged rain. The rocks should not have one joint above another lest a tunnel be formed for falling water. Also, the stones should tilt down in back toward the bank to catch the rainwater. The whole wall must be battered back slightly for the same purpose.

A good soil mix for laying between the rocks and pounding in behind is one third each of topsoil, sharp sand or fine gravel, and peat. If there is old manure available, add that, too—a shovelful or two to each bushel of the mix. If the wall is in the sun, add plenty of ground limestone, as some of the plants like it. Small stones chucked into this mixture are all to the good.

Try to plant as you go, laying the small plants horizontally in the pockets that are formed as you are about to lay one rock over the place where two others meet. As the wall garden becomes established, the plants will seed themselves into other crevices, so that it will really take care of itself. All you will have to do is pull out the occasional weed or superfluous self-seeded plants. If you are unable, for some reason, to plant the wall as it is being built, you can poke holes in the pockets later, insert small plants, and press soil over and around them. It's more difficult to get them started that way but not impossible.

If no handy slope needing a retaining wall exists on your property, the solution is to build a raised bed with stones, bricks, railway ties, or even planks and to fill it with the same mixtures given above. A stone bed can be constructed exactly like the retaining wall, with layers of soil between the stones and plants inserted in the pockets that occur as you lay each course. The walls should be battered back and the stones tilted slightly, just as in the planted retaining wall. You can, however, build the sides of the raised bed straight up, putting no soil between the layers, and plant everything on top. The mat formers will cascade down the side if planted near the edge. Largish stones should be tumbled in before filling the bed with the soil mixture, and the top of the bed should be mulched with small stone chips.

A raised bed can be of any shape that will harmonize with the site–round, rectangular, L-shaped, it doesn't matter. If the soil is well pounded in, most plants will do just as well in the raised bed as they would on a wall. And if it is artistically–that is, simply and beautifully–contrived, you and your plants will both enjoy it for a long time.

Many of the easier rock garden plants will grow well enough in the front of the border, but you are better off planting them in a rock garden, a wall garden, or a raised bed, any one of which isolates small plants from their smothering neighbors, provides sharp drainage for saxatile plants that require it (even raising such plants a few inches helps), and allows rock plants to display their natural, attractive growth habits. A wall garden even enables one to better observe the small subjects by bringing them closer to eye level: Miss Jekyll used to drag a chair out to her wall garden so that she could carefully and comfortably examine each plant. Further, planting vertically in a wall keeps water from settling in the crowns of sensitive plants during the winter, freezing and possibly killing them. Saxifrages, lewisias, and drabas, for instance, like to be vertical.

Let us now consider some rock plants that are not true alpines and may easily be grown in either wall or raised bed, and the ways they may be dealt with. If you are building a retaining wall or raised bed in the sun and it is only about two feet high, you will be confining yourself to smaller plants, such as drabas, the smaller sedums, sempervivums, and perhaps some different varieties of creeping thyme. Larger plants can go on top or here and there at the foot of the wall.

People seem to feel strongly either pro or con about sedums and sempervivums. I used to loathe them one and all, and I still feel uneasy, if not downright repelled, at the sight of blooming sempervivums, even after learning to admire them while they are just lying low being hens and chickens. There are some good ones with most interesting colors and textures. My favorite is one I bought as *S. arachnoideum hirsutum,* which weaves hairy webs across its rosettes, as one might guess from its name. And, I must admit, the flowers are a delicious shade of coral pink. I also have a large dark red sempervivum whose name I don't know. It looks very good with the silver *Cerastium tomentosum columnae.* If you're fond of gray or blue-green foliage, you'll love *Sedum sieboldii.* Its small thick round leaves are edged with pink, and it bears deep pink flowers in late summer. The stems all rise from the center of the plant, making a thick whorl. (A sedum of somewhat similar design, although not so dense, is *S.* 'Ruby Glow', but it is larger and should be used in the taller wall or raised bed.)

Armeria, or thrift, looks like a tight, grassy hummock. The species and cultivars of *A. maritima,* sometimes listed as *A. laucheana,* are fine for a high, gritty location. They come in various shades of hot pink or in white. But best of all, if you can find it, is *A. juniperifolia (caespitosa),* which is even more tightly packed and has flowers of a paler, classier pink. The leaves of this plant are shorter and wider than those of the more common *Armeria maritima.*

The double tunica is airy and graceful with its grassy foliage, and it really does bloom constantly, producing its tiny pink roses from spring to fall. Creeping baby's breath *(Gypsophila repens),* with single flowers of pink or white, is easy to raise from seed and another excellent candidate. Unlike its taller, bushier relative, it is long-lived and dependable and will usually rebloom if you shear it after its big burst in June.

Androsace sarmentosa makes furry spheres that send up two- to three-inch stems topped with pale pink, verbenalike flowers in spring. It spreads by above-ground stolons, like a strawberry, making colonies. *A. sempervivoides* resembles a succulent with its tight clusters of rosettes. Although they enjoy a gritty soil and plenty of light, neither of these androsaces wants to be cooked in the full afternoon sun.

Some of the smaller campanulas would be happy on a low wall: *C. garganica, C. portenschlagiana, C. raddeana,* and tiniest of all, *C. cochleariifolia (pusilla),* which wanders around putting forth miniature down-hanging bells in lavender-blue or white. If you put it on top of a wall, its roots will travel down so that its flowers will pop out from between the rocks.

Aubrieta behaves beautifully in such a situation—it's made to cascade. It comes in lovely colors, especially the 'Bengale' mixture, and spreads its low mats of pink, lavender, purple, or red-violet over a sizable area, blooming for a long time. *Antennaria dioica,* pussytoes (the pink one is pretty), loves a wall and could live on the top, spilling over if it liked. I would beware of the ordinary *Cerastium tomentosum* as being too aggressive, but *C.t. columnae* is admirably disciplined, confining itself to making a lovely low silver-white mat.

The perky little *Erinus alpinus* would probably seed itself around, once started. If it died during the winter, you would have its progeny, at any rate. I prefer *E.a.* 'Dr. Hähnle' (sometimes listed as 'Dr. Hanele') to the species, 'Dr. Hähnle' having minute hot-pink flowers and the species a kind of washed-out lavender. 'Dr. Hähnle' in a raised bed here this year bloomed from May to the middle of November. Small clumps of *Phlox subulata,* if carefully supervised, would be suitable and pretty, but this phlox is a great grabber; you must keep a sharp lookout lest it smother the other tenants of your wall. Cut the clumps back firmly after they finish blooming, and pull out pieces that are insufficiently cowed by cutting. Of course, nearly everything needs to be sheared back after blooming.

To contrast with the shapes of mound and mat formers, one could use dwarf iris as well as *Veronica alpina* 'Alba' and *V.* 'Heidekind'. Both veronicas bear their flowering spikes on low-growing plants.

On a sunny wall that is four or five feet or taller one would have a chance to use some of the larger plants that are really small shrubs: the stunning, pink-flowering aethionemas with their almost blue, succulent leaves; *Hebe decumbens,* also with succulent foliage and gray leaves edged with a thin red line; lavenders; santolinas; the dwarf ibiris; and silver or gold-edged thyme. Helianthemums, also called sun or rock roses, love living on a wall. Their blossoms do resemble those of wild roses and are especially beautiful with the sun shining through their translucent petals. Very pretty ones can be raised from seed, but the cultivars are even prettier. *Helianthemum apenninum* var. *roseum* has gray leaves and soft pink flowers, *H.* 'Fire Dragon' the same gray foliage combined with apricot blossoms. 'Rose Queen' comes in delicious deep pink with dark green leaves, and 'Wisley Primrose' is a long-blooming bright yellow. 'St. Mary's' has large white flowers. The double ones, such as 'Cerise Queen' (which is not cerise but rose) and 'Jubilee', a pale yellow, don't drop their petals at noon on a sunny day, as do most of the single ones. These named helianthemums are hybrids and cultivars of three species—*H. apenninum, H. nummularium,* and *H. croceum (glaucum).* There are many more named varieties than the ones I have mentioned.

Anemone pulsatilla, or pasqueflower, does better on a wall or raised bed than anywhere else, seeding itself with gusto (the same can be said for lavender). *Dianthus gratianopolitanus (caesius),* the cheddar pink, finds itself at home, especially on limestone rocks, spreading out its blue-green mats luxuriantly. *Dianthus deltoides* might attempt to take over with its seedlings, but you could try it. Perhaps you would be safer using a cultivar, such as *D.d.* 'Zing Rose', although it is not reliably hardy in the north. *Campanula carpatica* grows almost twice as big on a wall as on the level ground, and *C. poscharskyana* makes a lovely trailing clump. *C. rotundifolia* knows no restraint when it comes to producing young, and the same regrettable tendency is shown by a nice little round gray thing with white daisies, *Erigeron compositus.* But it's so beguiling you won't mind the chore of pulling out the extras.

Except for *Penstemon pinifolius,* a tiny broomlike shrub with violently vermilion tubular flowers, all of these sun-loving rock plants go well together, some of them having gray foliage and all of them bearing flowers of pink, white, lavender, blue, or pale yellow. A good neighbor for the hot little penstemon would be *Achillea tomentosa,* which has gray, woolly, flat foliage and deep yellow flowers (*A. lewisii* 'King Edward' is pale primrose yellow). Near those two could be *Anthemis marschalliana (biebersteiniana),* also with gray foliage and deep yellow daisies. *Archillea argentea* or *clavennae* could supply more silver foliage with pure white daisies. Add a blue creeping campanula flattened against the rocks, and what could be prettier?

If your wall or raised bed is in the shade—and it should not be close, gloomy shade—the soil should be a peaty, acid wood-soil mixture suited to plants that ordinarily feed on moist humus formed by rotting leaves. There are many plants that can be used to clothe a shady wall, although perhaps fewer than those that enjoy a rocky site in the sun. There's a fairly new *Ajuga,* 'Burgundy Glow', that looks like a strawberry dessert with cream on it. Its behavior is not rampant like that of other, more plebeian members of its family. The ferny, endlessly blooming *Corydalis lutea* and *C. ochroleuca,* which is even fernier and paler, love rocks and protection from the sun. Campanulas are tolerant of quite a bit of shade, and *Hutchinsia alpina* actually requires it. Edelweiss would be grateful to be saved from the blasting August heat. *Saxifraga umbrosa,* London pride, has foliage in the form of tight rosettes like those of a succulent, but its tiny pink or white flowers float above it on six- to eight-inch stems. It is not difficult to raise from seed and likes to have rocks packed around it. Certainly prim-roses, *Primula vulgaris* and *P. polyanthus,* would settle in at the foot of your shady wall if given good rich soil and plenty of moisture. You could even try the succulent-looking *P. auricula* in pockets on the wall itself. It grows in the full sun only where the air is cool and dry and likes lots of grit mixed with its soil.

What about some of our woodland natives? Hepatica sits directly on the flat stones by a stream in the woods near our house, its roots reaching out for the drifts of soil between layers of rock. Its dark green, three-lobed leaves are decorative all year round, and its pink, lavender, blue, or white flower heads bear clusters of starry stamens. Hepatica's silky-stemmed flowers emerge very early in spring. *Dode-catheon meadia,* shooting stars, would be suited to wall or raised bed, given a pocket of rich acid soil. The smooth, lance-shaped leaves of this plant stay close to the ground, but the leafless stems that hold the drooping umbels of blossoms may be eighteen inches tall. The sta-mens form a pointed beak from which the petals sweep upward like those of cyclamen. *Shortia galicifolia,* or oconee bells, is harder to please but worth trying: I have friends who have succeeded. The round glossy leaves and nodding white flowers on eight-inch stems are perfectly lovely. The four-inch blue and gold *Iris cristata* could be planted at the base of the wall, where it would spread its crablike rhizomes until it had formed a colony.

I put *Polemonium* 'Blue Pearl' in the partly shaded section of a raised bed last year, and it was the star of the show this spring. It stays low, unlike ordinary Jacob's ladder, and produces its delicate lavender-blue blossoms over a period of many weeks. A tiny alpine poppy with apricot-orange flowers just happened to be next to it, and I was given credit for the Cézanne color combination. 'Blue Pearl' doesn't seed itself and, having pinnately divided leaves that never turn yellow, is always attractive.

Cymbalaria muralis (Linaria cymbalaria), known also as Kenilworth ivy, is a delightful plant to use for draping a shady rock wall. It will seed itself in all the crevices and send its pretty little scalloped leaves and minute lavender labiate flowers foaming down over the rocks. It never seems to stop blooming. *C. pallida* has leaves and flowers of more substance and is also a nonstop bloomer. Some of the small new real ivies would also be perfect for a shady rock wall if your region is not too cold for them. *Mazus reptans* might like a wall—if you can get a tuft started, it would probably spread into a sheet in short order.

Some of the native ferns will also do well planted in a shady wall. The aspleniums are an example. *A. platyneuron*, the ebony spleenwort, grows to only eight inches and likes part shade and rocky soil. *Polypodium vulgare* prefers a rock crevice to all locations; there's one that's put itself between two of our stone front steps. The Japanese painted fern, *Athyrium nipponicum (goeringianum) pictum*, is handsomest of all ferns with its elegant combination of greens, grays, and dark wine red; it needs a rich moist soil and room in which to spread out. Try using it with dark red astilbes and the silvery gray *Ajuga* 'Silver Beauty'. *Ajuga metallica crispa* or *A.* 'Bronze Beauty' might be a nice addition— or what about *A.* 'Gaiety', which one catalog says has "glowing bronze-red foliage streaked and mottled with tan, cream, gold and copper tones"?

Before going fern wild, study the section on ferns in Lincoln Foster's *Rock Gardening* (which is finally in print again) so that you won't select the kinds that will take over your shade garden. And try planting golden moneywort (*Lysimachia nummularia* 'Aurea') so that it hangs down among the green ferns and yellow *Corydalis ochroleuca*.

There are now some six- to ten-inch hostas available that would be a great addition to a shady rock garden. I'm trying *H.* 'Rocknoll Dwarf Blue', which is of good dark dense foliage and has blue flowers. *H.* 'Louisa' has been around for a while and is really enchanting—eight to ten inches, with a white edge on the long, narrow leaf. The flowers are white and stand straight out from the stem like angels' trumpets on a Christmas card.

All the other plants under discussion are perennials, but I see no objection to using blue annual lobelia in the shady wall or *Phacelia campanularia,* whose deep gentian-blue flowers are displayed over a long period. Think how lovely they would be with the pale yellows.

For the more experienced gardener, or one with extra patience, the gorgeous blue creeping gromwell, now called *Lithodora diffusa* (formerly *Lithospermum diffusum*) 'Grace Ward,' is a thrilling addition to a woodsy area. It must be kept in soil that is rich, moist, peaty, and acid and covered with pine boughs in severe winter weather. It's a flat evergreen creeper that bears pure cobalt-blue cups in a sheet of color in spring. The same experienced gardener could try planting the native gaywings *(Polygala paucifolia)* near it, since they like the same conditions and the rosy purple fringed blossoms would be all the prettier near the blue gromwell. Polygala is hard to move, however: Mine seemed to pine for some mysterious, unidentified companion it had had in the woods. I moved it successfully by taking a very large clump of it, including all of its friends, and depositing it whole into a nice wide shallow nest I had prepared for it in the woods garden. It throve for several years but was eventually swamped by Virginia blue-bells.

If you are lucky enough to find *Thalictrum kiusianum,* which Foster calls the gem of the meadow rue tribe, make sure it doesn't get run over by its more aggressive neighbors or dug up by yourself during a burst of spring cleanup enthusiasm. The delicate little creature is only three inches tall and comes up very late in the season. There is a new goatsbeard on the market these days that stands about ten inches tall and couldn't be nicer—feathery, delicate, and re-strained. It's called *Aruncus aethusifolius.*

As for using bulbs in raised planting, I can't speak from experience because I grow bulbs in colonies in a small woods garden and around shrubs and trees. But why not try putting bulbs of scilla, puschkinia,

Papaver fauriei

. . . a rock garden, a wall garden, or a raised bed . . . allows plants to display their natural, attractive growth habits.

or chionodoxa in soil pockets in a shady wall? It would be ravishing if they made themselves at home and started to seed themselves about. Certainly groups of them, combined with the miniature daffodils, such as *Narcissus triandus* var. albus, would be lovely on the ground near the wall, as would patches of *Anemone blanda* 'White Splendor'. The blue European woods anemone *(Anemone nemorosa)* will seed itself everywhere once it gets started, and the lacy foliage is as pretty as the flowers.

Not all of these many rock garden plants are equally winter-hardy. In this region, where we suffer from ferocious winds and not infrequent temperatures of minus 20 degrees F., I need to cover with pine boughs only lavender, helianthemum, santolina, hebe, aethionema, lithodora, and *Anemone blanda*. An odd thing is that the rock plants that perch on top of a wall and get every wind that blows usually come through the winter better than the ones in the perennial border, where they are more protected—which seems to show how important drainage is in relation to winter hardiness.

Inevitably we find, in the spring, that there have been winter losses. Was the plant not hardy enough to endure the cold? Or was it encouraged by *warm* temperatures in March or April to start its new growth, then killed by a subsequent plunge of the thermometer? Did rodents destroy it? Was the drainage inadequate? If we ascertain the cause, we may avoid other losses. Keen gardeners learn to take such losses philosophically, in any event, and quickly console themselves with the thought that an empty spot gives them a place to try something new.

25

ON GARDENING

HERETOFORE IT WAS MOSTLY among the middle-aged that one found really gung-ho gardeners. This observation was not solely my own. May Sarton, for one, has this wonderful sentence in *Plant Dreaming Deep:* "Gardening is one of the rewards of middle age, when one is ready for an impersonal passion."

Then there was Colette. Her biographer, Margaret Crosland, said,

> *A passion for gardening is usually a sign of middle age, a kind of physical contact which one does not need earlier. Colette, who had a mysterious attachment to any form of living mat ter, could never forget her mother's love of plants, and in her garden was perfectly happy.**

Colette realized the therapeutic effect that gardening had upon her mother. She wrote in *Sido* that although her mother was a busy, bustling, proper housewife, she didn't really enjoy the assignment as

---

*Crosland, Margaret, *Colette.* New York: British Book Centre (1954).

some women do; she was clean and neat, but she got no pleasure from counting napkins or taking stock of provisions. A rough translation:

> *Cloth in hand, supervising the servant girl who was tediously mopping away at the windows and calling out to the neighbors, Sido would break into nervous cries that revealed her impatience for liberty. "When I wash and wipe my Chinese cups carefully for a long time," she said, "I can feel myself getting older." She stuck with the job dutifully until it was finished, then, crossing swiftly over the doorsill, went out into the garden. Suddenly her nervous depression and bitterness fell away from her. The presence of any kind of vegetation acted on her like an antidote. . . . She had a strange way of lifting up roses by the chin to look them straight in the face.†*

Crosland says that Colette herself became a "diabolical gardener" in her forties.

For those past their first youth it is undoubtedly true that spending time out-of-doors and dealing constantly with growing things can heal, to a great degree, feelings of rancor, anxiety, and regret. Of course, gardening is not enough; one needs more than the earth, the fragrance of vegetation, and the open sky, more even than flowers and the harmony of color, line, and form. But they are *almost* capable of "restoring the years the locust hath eaten."

There are, however, drawbacks to a belated realization of the joy of growing things. First, the gardener won't be around to see his garden, especially the trees he has planted, attain maturity. Nor does he have much time to profit from his experience; just when he begins to know quite a lot, it's time to leave. Finally, if he has no willing helpers, he takes on strenuous physical labor when he's beginning to

---

†Colette, *Sido.* Paris: J. Ferenczi & Fils (1930).

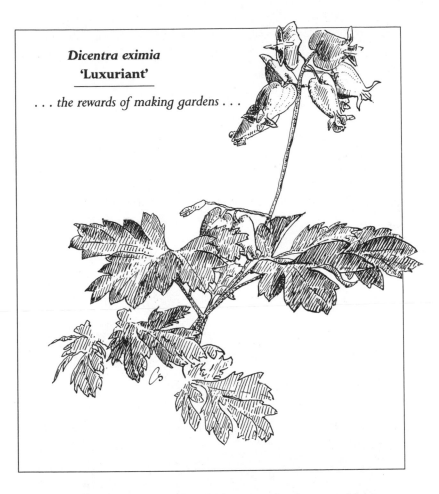

Dicentra eximia
'Luxuriant'

. . . the rewards of making gardens . . .

be a bit creaky, so the work, while tremendously enjoyable, is not always easy.

Hence one greets with gladness the evidence that young people are increasingly learning the rewards of making gardens. They will be embellishing the landscape for all of us while providing for themselves healthful exercise, aesthetic satisfaction, and the joy that anyone experiences while he is adding to his store of knowledge and accomplishments. They will also be finding a refuge, part of the time at least, from this fairly frightening world.

INDEX